Pat –
May God show you
how greatly He loves
you through these stories

Carrie Coffman

Also by Carrie S. Coffman

BREAKTHROUGH
A Prayer Journey through the Pacific

BORED READERS DON'T PRAY MUCH
Three Simple Steps to Writing Newsletters That Recruit Prayer

WEARY WARRIORS,
Lessons from Christian Workers Who Burned Out

Sweet Fire

Sweet Fire

Stories of God's Comfort
Experienced in Pain

Carrie Sydnor Coffman
with Mary Lou Sather

Foreword by Dr. Dan Allender

Majesty Publishers · Leesburg, Virginia

For additional copies, contact: Majesty Publishers
P.O. Box 1623
Leesburg, VA 20177
(703) 669-6737
Fax: (703) 669-6738
majestypub@adelphia.net
www.majestypublishers.com

Published by Majesty Publishers.

Cover designed by Kathy Walker.

ISBN 0-9633283-4-4
Printed in the United States of America by Lightning Source.
First Edition

"Hard times experienced with God
are no longer just difficulties.
They are sweet fire."

—Helene Catoire of France

Dedicated to my siblings—
Gleaves, Sarah, Jeannie, and Bucky—
who have brought me a great deal of comfort
in my widowhood.

About the Authors

"Can you write?" a woman asked Carrie Sydnor, age 26, at a summer training program in Nebraska, for Christian college students.

"Yes," answered Carrie, who had quit her job as a computer programmer to lead a women's team there.

"Well, the city newspaper wants a two-page article about what we're doing here. Could you please write it?"

The resulting newspaper clipping landed on the desk of the vice president of The Navigators, an international Christian organization. Two years later that vice president was asked to find a writer to move to Kuala Lumpur, Malaysia to write about what God was doing in Asia. On the basis of that one article, he asked Carrie.

Interestingly, she did not want to go to that training program because of its reputation for mosquitoes, heat, humidity, and bad food. But in obedience to God's leading, she had gone. The decision led her into a fascinating career she could not have found herself.

After four years of traveling in Asia, Carrie, a graduate of Duke University, enhanced her skills at the University of Missouri School of Journalism and returned to Asia for a year. Later she spent four years in Nairobi, Kenya, this time writing about God at work in Africa. For ever since Christ filled her empty heart and gave her a burning purpose at age nineteen, she longed to play a vital part in spreading the good news about Christ globally.

Moving to California after Africa, she received some junk mail from a secular dating agency and filled out a questionnaire on a lark about the kind of man she would like to marry. As a result, she met and married Colonel (ret) King Coffman in 1989. They spent six years in Moscow, pioneering a Christian outreach to Russian military officers and their wives. Since then that work has spread to sixty-eight cities stretching across nine time zones. Soon after the Coffmans returned home in 1998, King died from a life-long lung condition.

Today Carrie lives in Leesburg, Virginia, near her husband's grandchildren in order to play a part in imparting biblical values into their lives. And, at last, she can focus on writing books that she's been dying to write for years.

*

Mary Lou Sather wrote her first book when she was eight years old. A graduate of the University of Minnesota, she has been a writer and editor for many years. Her work includes construction, ghostwriting and copyediting for a number of memoirs, biography/autobiographies, science textbooks, theological works, and other non-fiction. She has also published over two hundred magazine articles covering a wide range of subjects.

She lives in Minneapolis near two of her three children. To her great joy, her six grandchildren all are excited about writing.

Author's Note

As a missionary journalist for nine years, I found myself often interviewing godly people. A friend pointed out that I could get away with asking direct questions that others couldn't ask. Whatever interested me, I would inquire about it. I especially wanted to know how the Lord met these people during painful times in their lives as I longed to taste God's comfort in areas where I still hurt.

Then in 1993 I saw a friend from years ago whose teenage daughter had committed suicide. We cried together as she shared the depth of her pain and the reality of God's comfort. Her story prompted me to make a list of moving stories about God's comfort which I'd heard over the years as I interviewed people. The idea for this book took shape that week.

The stories written in this book cover a wide range of pain—death of a loved one, anger, tragic accident, marital problems, addiction. The way God comforted each of these people is unique since the Lord relates to each of His children in an individual and personal manner.

No one but Moses had God speak to him through a burning bush. However, God did speak to him. Moses knew He spoke to him. And God did answer all of Moses' questions. We can learn principles and lessons from Moses' encounter with God although we will probably never experience God speaking to us through a burning bush.

Likewise, these stories of how God comforted people all contain principles and lessons that hold just as true for us when we suffer and desperately need God's touch. Yet we should avoid making the mistake of expecting God to heal our hurts in the same way that He did for the characters in these chapters.

All the stories moved me deeply; that's why I chose to write them. Yet I have found that different people react differently to each incident because we all read them with a backdrop of our own experiences and concerns. Therefore, if one chapter does not appeal to you, just jump to the next.

The stories in this book are all true. The people interviewed each read the chapter about them (at least one draft), made corrections and gave me permission to print what happened to them.

One chapter is about me. To keep from confusing you, I refer to myself in the third person.

When I suffer, hearing how God has comforted other people gives me hope. Frequently, the truths they learned and the Scriptures that moved them percolate in my mind and speak powerfully to my need, too.

I pray that the Lord will do the same for you as you read this book.

Carrie Coffman
August 2003
Leesburg, Virginia

Acknowledgements

My thanks begin with my mother Caroline Sydnor on numerous fronts. I grew up hearing her enthrall people with good stories. She instinctively knew what to leave out and what would captivate her listeners. Watching her do that made an impact on me as a future storyteller.

Plus she modeled for me a standard of excellence in whatever she did. She had a can-do spirit, writing five books about the card game of bridge and marketing them herself. Two of them won awards. Her entrepreneurial spirit proved contagious, and now I'm writing and marketing the books I write.

As I've interviewed people for this book, time and time again they chose courageously to reveal the depth and details of their pain in hopes of helping others. There would be no book without them.

Joy George, Carol Reusser, Fereva Kaiserman, Tom Steers and Trudie Crawford read the initial manuscript and gave me honest feedback. They steered me in the right direction.

Esther Waldrop edited half the book until her fifth pregnancy plus living overseas made it impossible to continue. She taught me a lot.

Kathy Walker did her magic to produce the book cover. Mary Lou Sather turned my newspaper style into a literary style, enhancing the readability of the book. Madeline Trotman convinced me to add at the end of each chapter a section spotlighting the gold that people gained in their lives as a result of the pain they went through. Larry Seskes volunteered to proofread my work, saving me from a lot of embarrassment. Joy George combed through the final manuscript, alerting me to many needed changes. Andy Burt taught me how to place the photographs in the text on my computer and how to make an index with my software.

And if it were not for the Russian Military Christian Fellowship that my late husband founded, *Sweet Fire* would still be only an idea. Their need for finances until they can fund their own ministry drove me to tackle this book at this time.

Then, of course, I want to thank the Lord who gifted me as a writer, who gave me the idea for this book, who created in me a burning desire to comfort others and who gave me the perseverance needed to make *Sweet Fire* a reality.

And if God did not give incredible comfort to hurting people who cry out to Him, there would be no book to write on this topic. For that phenomenal trait, I can never praise Him enough.

Foreword

I have had the privilege of watching my friend Carrie Coffman wrestle with her own personal demons and receive a wonderful peace. I've seen her question whether she would ever know the love of a husband, and then seen her know not only sweet love, but a ministry with her beloved that grew to have an enormous impact. I've also watched her suffer the loss of her husband. In all those moments, I have always been moved by her honesty, depth of faith, and willingness to plunge deeper into reality than most mere mortals. She is a woman of God—a plucky, passionate, rare soul that presses to know the exquisite comfort of our great Abba.

Comfort is desired only to the degree we know its absence. It is before the cruel and piercing wet winds of life that the down-jacket comforts of this world fall away as ineffective and useless. Don't talk to me of God's comfort unless you've been bled raw by the slings and arrows of outrageous fortune. Even then, to speak of what we know is true about God's comfort can come across as insipid—perhaps true, but unmoving. It is rare that by talking about comfort, one feels the sweet, gentle arms of God.

There is simply nothing my heart wants more than God's comfort—and nothing harder to communicate to someone in the middle of agony. As difficult as that may be, it is even harder to proffer the glory of His care to someone who currently is docile and satisfied in the arms of sufficient material and interpersonal blessing. To those who ache it is too far away and to those who are satisfied, it is presumed and ignored. In either case, it requires two qualities to break through the fog.

First, it requires a writer who knows heartache and the intermittent periods of hope that come without demand or presumption. Carrie has lived with despair and joy and has come to know the presence of His comfort in both extremes. There is no better person to have taken on this terrible and awesome task.

Second, the need for and the provision of comfort is best inscribed, perhaps incarnated through story. Carrie's life has been a long, faithful journey into the heart of darkness and light through thousands of lives. She has the unique capacity to disarm the defensive and enter the small cracks in the human psyche to hear the heartache and draw forth the desire for God. She has traveled the world and has supped with many whose stories she tells with winsome and sweet glory.

Carrie draws my heart to consider the depth of both my

poverty and need and the wonder of what I've already known and might know in even richer fare if I hear the life-giving call of my God to sink into His arms. Comfort is truly only a grief away, if I turn and rush to the One who catches each tear, bottles it, and wipes away the tracks with His nail-marked hands.

What I invite you to in this book is a feast. Take off your shoes. Open your heart. Sit before the throne of God, and be stunned at how our Father longs to serve you as a host, giving us His comfort through His bread and wine, His body and His very blood. His comfort is yours; partake and read with joy.

Dan B. Allender, Ph.D.
President
Mars Hill Graduate School

Contents

Disclaimer

This book is designed to provide encouragement that God does, in fact, comfort His people in a concrete way. It is sold with the understanding that the publisher and author are not engaged in rendering professional counseling services. If assistance is needed to deal with a particular area of need, the reader can seek competent, professional help.

Every effort has been made to make this book as accurate as possible—both in the details of the stories and in the reliability of the advice offered. However, there may be errors in content or in judgment. Therefore, this text should be used as a general guide and not as the ultimate source on how to access God's comfort.

The purpose of this book is to give hope and show practical ways that God has comforted people in a wide range of crises. The author and publisher shall have neither liability nor responsibility to any person or entity with respect to any loss or damage caused or alleged to be caused directly or indirectly by applying the information contained in this book.

If you do not wish to be bound by the above, you may return this book to the publisher for a full refund of the price of the book.

Part I

Turmoil

Chapter One

THE MAN
WITH THE SHORT FUSE

Carolyn Repko carefully threaded her way toward the airport through the thick traffic. Up ahead, she spotted her husband Denny standing on the curb, having just returned from a work-related trip. As she pulled into a handy parking space right in front of her, Denny gestured to another parking spot closer to him. But that spot seemed smaller and the traffic was heavy, so she stayed where she was. Fuming, Denny strode over, threw his bags into the car and climbed in beside her. To display his displeasure, he did not even greet her or speak a single word all the way home.

Although his friends and associates did not know this side of Denny, Carolyn and their four children knew it well. Sometimes when he came home, a black cloud came into the house with him and everyone in the family would become tense . . . tiptoeing around in order to avoid displeasing him and then getting scolded.

After one trip, Denny walked in the door and saw his four children sitting on the floor playing cards. Eleven-year-old Greg had asked his mother a few days earlier if he could buy a deck of playing cards. Carolyn couldn't think of any reason why not, and gave her permission. Denny, however, had grown up in a very conservative Christian family that considered playing cards a sin. Seeing his children sitting there with those terrible pieces of cardboard in their hands, he was livid, especially at his wife for having been so foolish as to permit such unseemly conduct in his very house.

He called an immediate family meeting to discuss the matter. Assuming his heaviest air of authority, he began to lecture them all, conjuring up every reason he could think of to show how serious this sin was. The children, ages four to eleven, listened with tears in their eyes.

After the lecture, six-year-old Lisa asked meekly, "What's the matter with playing cards?"

Totally unprepared for this innocent question, Denny began to bluster. "I cannot think of a single Christian leader who plays cards!"

Sniffling through her tears, Lisa countered: "Well, Greg is no Christian leader." The entire family burst out laughing, including Denny. The lecture ended, and the Repko family has played cards peacefully ever since.

Denny had worked as a Christian leader in Sweden and England and now travels extensively from his home in California to lead seminars for Christian groups in Europe and Asia. People all over the world admired him as a lively, stimulating, unpretentious servant of God. They enjoyed his winsome, outgoing personality. The other Denny, the one known only to his family, stayed carefully under cover.

But God was getting ready to confront Denny about his anger.

Three men from the Repkos' church invited him to join them for a weekly Bible study. Denny felt privileged to be asked to join these successful, professional men—a prominent dentist and two prosperous real estate brokers—and his self-esteem soared. They met once a week over lunch in a back room at the dentist's office, spending an hour and a half or more, discussing the Scriptures and sharing with one another.

Initially they had intended to meet for only a year or so, but as the bonds of friendship grew, the meetings continued. After a few years, Denny's infatuation with the group began to wear off. *I can't brag in my reports to my supervisor about what I am accomplishing by meeting with them,* he thought. *The get-togethers give no credit to my ministry.* So he told Carolyn, "I think it's time for me to move on and leave the Bible study with these guys from church."

"No," she said in her usual soft manner. "You need those men in your life." He sensed the Lord speaking to him through her and changed his mind.

Three years later as Denny drove home after one of their sessions, he prayed, "Lord, why is this group of men so important to me?" Suddenly he realized that as love had grown between them, they now felt safe enough to be transparent with one another. As each one talked openly about what was really going on in his heart and life, the other men would insist that he live up to their agreed standards and they all would check up on one another.

One day as they shared their prayer requests for the week, without any thought beforehand Denny asked, "Hey, would you guys pray that I could lose weight? I want to get down to what I weighed in college before Carolyn and I take a trip for our twenty-fifth wedding anniversary."

Frowning, Dave said, "I'm sick and tired of praying about people's weight!" He pulled out his notebook. With pen poised, he asked, "How much weight do you want to lose, Denny?" Then he added, "By when?" He paused. "And what will be the consequences that you'll agree to if you don't make your goal?"

Time stopped. It was a significant moment. Denny thought, *Wait a minute. I don't want to be held accountable. I just want sympathy and prayer.*

But Dave was going on. "I'll tell you the consequences. If you don't make your goal, you'll take the three of us out to dinner at a restaurant of OUR choice."

Immediately Denny thought of his humble Volkswagen parked near their three expensive cars in the parking lot. He could picture what kind of restaurant they'd choose.

Trying to figure out what he'd gotten himself into, he asked, "What will you guys do if I make my goal?"

"Nothing," Dave replied. "It's your goal."

The group had reached a milestone. The men had become utterly honest friends to each other, manifesting signs of love, transparency and almost fierce accountability.

Denny did lose his weight in time, but barely; he had to fast the last two days before the deadline. The whole experience taught Denny a major lesson about the power of being a good friend: "When we lack courage to hold a friend accountable as those men did to me, we compromise what the Lord wants to do in that person's life."

A few months later, just as the four men began sharing their prayer requests again, the Holy Spirit tapped Denny on the shoulder and distinctly spoke to his heart, *I have news for you. You have a problem with anger.* Astounded, he silently asked the Lord, *Who? Me? Nice-guy Denny?*

Yes, I mean you, God's Spirit continued. *Not only are you an angry person, but you're also an angry husband. You're an angry father. And just in case you don't get the point, you're even an angry Christian worker!*

An angry Christian worker! To hear that hurt the most. For Denny had always striven to live in a way that wouldn't bring disrepute on the Lord or the Christian organization for which he worked.

After catching his breath, Denny told the group, "The Lord just showed me that I have a problem with anger." And he asked them to pray for him.

"OK," said Dave, the action man. "What are you going to do about it?" This time Dave's pointed questions didn't surprise Denny. *This is one of those divine moments,* he thought. He could see that Dave was facilitating the Holy Spirit's work by acting out Ephesians 4:15—

*Speaking the truth in love,
we will in all things grow up into . . . Christ.*

Miserably Denny sought an answer. "I don't know," he said, "but I guess I can begin by confessing my anger to my family."

Rather than stew in anguish all week, Denny took Carolyn and their two sons, ages seventeen and twenty-four, out to dinner that very night. Their two daughters, away at college, missed this momentous occasion. As the four of them were eating dessert, Denny cleared his throat and said, "The Lord has shown me today that I'm an angry person, an angry husband, an angry dad and an angry Christian worker. Will you all forgive me?"

Twenty-four-year old Greg was sitting across the table from his father. He stared back at him, eyes wide in disbelief. Denny's discovery came as no surprise to the rest of the family. They'd been well aware of his smoldering anger for many years. In fact, the children had been conscious of it all their lives.

Denny could see that he'd acquired this pattern from childhood. In the community where he grew up, people strove to work hard and to look good. Parents felt they knew best; they held final authority. Some used anger to produce the desired behavior in their children because of what others might think. *We know better,* they seemed to say beneath their fury.

So all through Denny's adult years, he had remained truly unaware of what he was doing to those he loved most. Carolyn explains it this way: "An angry husband and father often feels that he's just shaping up his family and exercising his rightful biblical role."

As the Repkos sat together at that restaurant table, they knew that this amazing admission wouldn't solve the problem. It was only the first of many confessions of anger that Denny would have to make as time passed. However, what his honesty did do was raise his awareness level. After that, he could no longer easily slide over his anger or excuse it, for now he could recognize it more readily. The Holy Spirit had made a breakthrough.

Two weeks later it was Denny's turn to stand amazed at what God was doing in the heart of someone in the family. His son Greg asked his dad, "Would you pray for me about my anger?" The father's choice to do right was impacting his son—what every Christian parent longs for.

Twenty years have passed since that eventful dinner at the restaurant. Denny has come to agree with psychologist Larry Crabb that anger often signals a blocked goal in the individual's life. That might explain what's really going on, but Denny knows that it doesn't excuse his behavior. He's come to view 1 Corinthians 10:13 as the ultimate verse on dealing with his temptation to get angry—

> *No temptation has seized you*
> *except what is common to man.*
> *And God is faithful;*
> *he will not let you be tempted*
> *beyond what you can bear.*
> *But when you are tempted,*
> *he will also provide a way out*
> *so that you can stand up under it.*

"Look for a way out," Denny says. "It's always there. You just have to look for it. Anytime you have the calm sense to look, regardless of the temptation, there *is* a way to escape. This is not ethereal, it's real."

Recently he and Carolyn were eating at a local restaurant. They waited and waited and waited some more for their food to arrive. Denny hates inefficiency and he recognized that here was an instance when his anger could boil over. Nevertheless, taking the obvious "way out," he purposed before the Lord to control his feelings and continued to be pleasant to their waitress.

Not long before, he and Carolyn had spent their vacation in Seattle, visiting their daughter Tanya and her family. They badly needed a new shower stall, and Denny volunteered to help his son-in-law work on the project. Unexpectedly, it ended up absorbing all of Denny's time during the Repkos' visit, which was supposed to be a restful vacation.

About the third day, as Tanya and Carolyn left the house to go out and enjoy themselves, Tanya said, "Are you OK, Dad? We'll see you later." Left alone working on the shower stall, Denny realized that for the past few days anger had been slowly simmering in his heart. *They're out having fun, leaving me here alone to work,* he complained silently. Rather than gnashing his teeth, he acknowledged his anger to himself and confessed it to the Lord. No one else had any idea what had transpired.

Through his years of struggle, Denny has learned many lessons about what makes a person explode. "A man uses anger to control his family and others," he says. "He can be furious without even raising his voice or striking anyone. The children know what they can get by with as they watch Dad's body language, and they also know when they'd better shape up.

Carolyn and Denny Repko in 2000.

"Instead of being reasonable and constructive in the way a husband

and father exercises his leadership role, his angry outbursts are often cheap shots and shortcuts to get his desired results by intimidation. But by using these methods he frequently diminishes himself in the eyes of his wife and children."

Denny has also come to see how anger affects the relationship between a husband and his wife. He recalls hearing an analogy about the emotional bank account in a marriage. "You deposit grace into the account when you do something kind for your wife," says Denny. "But you take 'money' out when you get mad at her. Your angry words slowly deplete the account, and your wife's respect for you begins to slip away. Your marriage may not even survive."

At times Denny has felt that he wasn't making any progress at all in overcoming his anger. Then one day he read a quotation by Oswald Chambers, saying that a person obtains sanctification through many confessions. Those words enabled Denny to hold on and believe that he *could* change, but that the pathway to sanctification would come only through asking the Lord for forgiveness each time he failed.

So he plods onward in his battle against anger.

Recently a car ran a stoplight and pulled out in front of Denny's car. He flashed his lights at the driver and did not slow down, intending to give him a scare. "At the time it didn't seem like a big deal," says Denny. "I wasn't driving fast enough for it to be dangerous." However, the next morning he learned that Carolyn had seen it as evidence of anger, and he asked for forgiveness for making her feel uncomfortable.

"I feel like a pilgrim," he says, "just getting out of

kindergarten where overcoming my anger is concerned."

Meanwhile, his awareness of his own struggle has opened his eyes to similar situations in others' lives: "I see men whose anger is really a serious problem. It's decimating their families."

Yet if it were not for the group of men who met for twelve years in the back of the dentist's office, Denny would not have made strides in dealing with his own anger. Perhaps he would even have remained unaware of it. "Men need other men to hold them accountable in order to live for God," he says with deep conviction.

* * *

At times Denny vividly remembers the sting he felt that day when the Holy Spirit told him that he was an angry man . . . the humiliation before his family and the men in his accountability group . . . and the discouragement he has tasted when he has become angry time and time again. However, all this seems small indeed compared to the overwhelming benefits that have come his way on his journey to conquer his anger:

No one in his family walks on eggshells around him anymore. His children have had a powerful role model in humility and dealing with personal, continuing sin. The impact of this witness on his family and others around him is incalculable.

As Denny travels and speaks before groups in various countries, he naturally shares his life. This is just his style. Countless times while listening to Denny speak, men have come face to face with how their anger is tearing their own families apart. And men all over the world are learning why they, too, need transparent male friends who care enough to hold one another accountable.

Thus, God keeps getting mileage out of the brief and pointed confrontation He had with one of His children on an ordinary day.

Chapter Two

THE SPHINX AND HIS WIFE

Theresa and Scott James had been married for several years and the marriage was a good one by all outward appearances. However, as the years passed, Theresa found herself increasingly frustrated because whenever she wanted to share with Scott the exciting things God was teaching her, she couldn't find a way to tell him. She would be pouring her heart out to a girlfriend and suddenly realize that Scott had no knowledge of these important facets of her life.

Before Scott and Theresa had become engaged, they'd discussed what couples wanted most in marriage. Theresa had read an intriguing book—*His Needs/Her Needs: How to Have an Affair-Proof Marriage* by Dr. Willard Harley. And the author said that, based on his experience in counseling more than three thousand couples, he'd found five things which nearly every man wants from his wife . . . and five different things which most women want from their husbands. Amazingly, these were usually true of men and women regardless of culture, economic status or age. According to Dr. Harley, if all these needs are met in a marriage, the couple is protected from extramarital affairs and usually ceases to feel a need to keep seeing a counselor.

As Scott and Theresa[1] discussed the book at that time, they both admitted that the list of five things for the man and the woman were exactly what they themselves wanted in marriage.

"Wouldn't it produce an incredible marriage," Theresa had suddenly said, "if a wife said to her husband, 'I commit myself to you to make it a high priority to give you your five needs'. . . and if the man then said to his wife, 'I commit myself to you to devote myself to giving you your five things, too.'"

And as Scott and Theresa James moved toward marriage, they decided to make giving each other their "five things" a major goal in their relationship.

Scott was a very focused man. If he were in the middle of reading an article or sending e-mail at the moment that Theresa interrupted him to share something, he would become irritated. To him it seemed the height of arrogance that her agenda should supersede his on the spur of the moment. So Theresa's attempts to communicate with him were becoming a point of conflict between them.

At last they agreed that whenever she wanted to tell him something, she'd say, "When you're at a good stopping point, let me know because I have something I want

---

[1] Not their real names.

to share with you." Yet somehow she could never find a
way to tell him about her big lessons from God that took
more than three minutes to communicate.

She would try to initiate a discussion about what the
Lord was teaching her at dinnertime. But he seemed not to
hear her. He didn't respond in any way—not with a grunt,
not with a change in expression, not even an "uh-hum."

Am I boring? she wondered. She asked him on several
occasions if that were the case and he always said no. *But
if I'm not boring, why such a silent response to my attempts at
conversation?* she'd ask herself.

The days passed, and one night when Scott was weighed
down with problems from his business, she began to tell
him something with great excitement. To her frustration,
he didn't even look up from his food. The silence was overwhelming, but she comforted herself, thinking, *He is sooo
tired.* Believing that, she didn't have to face the pain of his
refusal to relate to her. Then, five minutes later he began
talking about some new, exciting development at the
office, going on and on about it. Theresa thought, *He has
time and energy to talk about what he wants to talk about, but
not about the major things that interest or concern me.*

Then one day, two old friends of theirs from years past
came to New York City on business and stayed with Scott
and Theresa for a few days. Over the weekend, Scott and
one of the men took off for the hardware store to find
some item for a project they were working on. This left
Theresa and the other man at home for thirty minutes and
they became involved in a conversation in the living room.
She told Dave something she was learning and to her utter
amazement and joy, he entered into the discussion. He connected mentally with what she was saying and responded

with his own thoughts. They continued their conversation for twenty minutes and Theresa was astonished at the way this simple exchange had refreshed her.

Long after the two visitors left New York for home, Theresa found herself daydreaming about Dave. She struggled with fantasies: *When Scott dies and when Dave's wife dies, maybe we could marry each other*, she would think. The fantasies shocked her. *This is ridiculous*, she told herself. She prayed daily that God would enable her to bring her thoughts into captivity to Christ.[2] Yet she couldn't suppress her recurring longing that she and Dave could someday be married.

Suddenly she recalled the book *His Needs/Her Needs* that she and Scott had discussed before their engagement. The author had observed that if a person is missing just one thing on the list of the five qualities that he needs from his spouse, he is vulnerable to having an affair.[3]

Men long for their wives to admire them; that's one of the five items on a husband's list. If his wife gives him everything else he wants—good sex, an attractive appearance, warm support when he comes home—but doesn't express her admiration for him, the time may come when his unattractive secretary who admires him, catches his attention in a new way. He may soon find himself tempted to proposition her.

These insights showed Theresa why she kept fantasiz-

---

[2]   2 Corinthians 10:5.

[3]   According to Dr. Willard Harley, author of *His Need/Her Needs — How to Have an Affair-Proof Marriage*, a man most longs for sexual fulfillment, recreational companionship, an attractive spouse, domestic support, and admiration in his marriage. A wife longs for affection, conversation, honesty and openness, financial security, and family commitment.

ing about marrying Dave in the future. Conversation is one of the five needs a woman longs to have satisfied in marriage, according to Dr. Harley. Dave had given her a taste of what it would be like to be able to have meaningful conversation with a man. So now Theresa concluded that she must confront her husband.

Usually Scott and Theresa resolved their conflicts in a mature fashion. He'd bring up something that was bothering him, or she would. Most of the time they could discuss their differences in a reasonable tone of voice. They both knew that the other one really wanted to do the right thing before God. The offended one needed only to define the problem simply. Then Scott could think about what he'd done wrong and Theresa could look at where she'd erred . . . instead of both of them hammering each other about the ways the other one had failed.

Although sometimes these discussions became a bit heated, almost always one or both of them would say, "Honey, you're right. It was really wrong of me to do that. Will you forgive me?" The apology might come a few hours later or even the next morning. So Theresa felt sure Scott would understand. After all, he knew that a woman longs for conversation in marriage, and they had decided years before to make a priority of giving each other the five desires that Dr. Harley had outlined in his book.

However, to her surprise, when she explained to Scott that she longed to be able to share with him at length what she was thinking about, he responded angrily: "If you insist on all this talking, I may start staying away from home more and more and you won't even know why. Then one day I might not come home at all." His words terrified her and caused her to retreat into silence about the issue.

Theresa then gave up trying to share with Scott anything of depth that she was learning. If she spoke briefly about something important to her, he responded briefly. But sharing for just two minutes didn't satisfy her deep longings for meaningful communication. *If we're going to have conversation in our marriage,* she realized, *I have to be available to talk about whatever he wants to discuss whenever he's in the mood.* She began stopping immediately whatever she was doing at those moments when he started to open up about some issue on his mind. And Theresa basically lost hope of ever having times of relating with Scott about what was going on in her life below the surface.

One day she realized, *Hey, I prayed for a husband with certain attributes and God gave me such a man. There's no rule that I can't trust God to move in Scott's heart to give him one more quality that I want.* So she began praying. Day after day, month after month, she asked God to do a work in Scott's heart so that he'd connect with her mentally and emotionally when she shared her thoughts, and would even be interested enough to want to discuss the topic. It seemed just too impossible to expect, and to assuage her pain and loneliness she would try to think of plausible reasons for his conduct. Yet she didn't give up because she knew Matthew 7:7 to be true—

> *Ask and keep asking, and you will receive.*
> *Seek and keep seeking, and you will find.*
> *Knock and keep knocking, and the door will be opened to you.*
> (literal meaning of the original Greek text)

Meanwhile, she could see that God was using this trial in a positive way in her life. She met with a close friend once a month and they could discuss at length whatever issues they were wrestling with. But from day to day, Theresa's only outlet for sharing her deepest thoughts was God Himself, and this enhanced her walk with Him.

One morning, as she struggled with the pain of one more silent response from Scott when she dared to try to tell him something that had been meaningful to her, she came across Proverbs 13:4—

The desires of the diligent are fully satisfied.

She was a hard worker and she knew this promise applied to her. The words gave her courage to believe that one day God would actually give her what she longed for in her marriage.

A year after her initial attempt to confront Scott about the lack of meaningful conversation in their marriage, a day came when she received a wonderful letter from an old college friend. Scott walked into the bedroom as she was reading it and she began to read it to him. He seemed to listen momentarily, but left the room two minutes later to go take care of his e-mail. The whole letter would have taken her no more than five or six minutes to read. Pain shot through her heart and she knew she wouldn't be able to sleep that night until she spent some time with the Lord. As she prayed about it at the end of the day, she remembered Proverbs 28:1—

The righteous are as bold as a lion.

A thought came to her: *Scott makes appointments with everybody else. I can ask him for an appointment to bring up this scary subject again.* But the piercing memory of his threat to leave her if she insisted on conversation shook her to the core.

The next evening she gathered the courage she'd been trusting God to give her, walked over to his side of the bed, sat down beside him and said, "I'd like to make an appointment with you to have a discussion."

"You get to talk to me every day," he countered.

"No, I want a time when you're not reading or distracted."

"If this is to lampoon me, it'll be the last time." Despite the pain his words caused, she forced herself not to stand up and leave.

"I don't intend to lampoon you, Honey. Where's your appointment book? I want you to write it down."

"It's in the office," he answered reluctantly. She went to get it and asked him to write in his own handwriting the time he'd like to meet with her. They agreed on four o'clock Saturday afternoon. It was now Wednesday.

His reaction increased her fears and being emotionally upset always gave her insomnia. So she spent three hours alone with the Lord that night—thinking, praying, reading the Scriptures. Just before she finally crawled into bed at one in the morning, she prayed, *Lord, please greatly encourage me tomorrow. I feel so vulnerable.*

The next day she started to pull every lever of power that she knew. She sent a lengthy e-mail to two close friends whom she could trust to keep the matter confidential, asking them to saturate Saturday's discussion in prayer. She wanted still more people to pray, but whom could she confide in? Her husband was highly respected in his company and at their church, so she dared not tell anyone else.

Knowing that Jesus Himself prays for us at the right hand
of God,[4] she asked Him to pray for the discussion on
Saturday, too.

A year earlier, God had revealed to Theresa a major
insight after one particularly painful encounter with Scott:
The real enemy was not her husband, but Satan. Scripture
says it pointedly, but she had never grasped the idea over
the years because it seemed so hard to believe:

We wrestle not against flesh and blood,
but against . . . spiritual wickedness in high places.
Ephesians 6:12 KJV

Therefore, as she prayed about her appointment with Scott
on the coming Saturday, she commanded Satan in the name
of Jesus Christ not to influence her husband in any way
during their discussion. Previously she'd found that com-
manding Satan verbally proved to be a highly effective way
of dealing with difficult or threatening people. She also
asked God to free Scott from any fear and dread of their
planned discussion. King David's example gave her hope
that God would answer her:

I sought the Lord and he answered me;
he delivered me from all my fears.
Psalm 34:4

That evening when Scott came home from work, he
walked into her study and lingered, talking to her for a
long time. The conversation was so refreshing that she

---

[4] Hebrews 7:25

wondered if he'd figured out what she wanted to talk to him about on Saturday. She tried again to share with him the wonderful letter from her college friend and this time he showed interest and listened to the whole story. Her two friends whom she'd e-mailed the previous day had obviously already started praying.

At dinner, Theresa and Scott had an unusually honest conversation for two hours. They both frankly shared negative thoughts they'd had about their marriage that they'd never told each other before. She sat stunned and suddenly realized, *God is doing what I prayed last night — that He would greatly encourage me today.* The telephone interrupted their discussion several times, but after each call, Scott returned to the dinner table to continue their conversation. Although he'd set the kitchen timer to remind himself to make an important phone call at a certain time, he ignored the timer when it went off. She could not remember a single day in recent years when they'd sat and talked for a full two hours about anything.

Scott finally rose to leave the dining room, but turned in the doorway and wagged his finger at her, saying, "If you rake me over the coals Saturday, it'll be the last time."

"Honey, I'm not going to rake you over the coals," she assured him.

His words shot through her with fear. *What constitutes "raking him over the coals?"* she wondered. *How can a woman approach her husband to have a needed conversation about a way that he's offending her if this is not allowed? Did this threat mean that he'd leave me? Or that he wouldn't agree to long, pre-scheduled talks in the future?*

Saturday morning Theresa awoke with but one agenda—to arm herself with all the Lord's resources available to her for the four o'clock appointment. Having experienced significantly increased power from fasting and praying in the past, she decided to eat nothing, drinking only water until after their discussion. Then she spent two hours thinking, praying, and writing down promises from the Scriptures that she was trusting God to fulfill. Her heart cried out to her heavenly Father that He would soften Scott's heart to be reasonable, to understand, and to want to meet her need for regular, meaningful conversation.

She also claimed God's promises for herself as a safeguard, such as:

[He] is able to keep you from falling.
Jude 24

For she could easily lose her temper with Scott if he turned ugly, and that would ruin everything. On the contrary, if Scott became testy, her behavior could salvage the situation. For she knew Proverbs 15:1—

A gentle answer turns away wrath.

She prayed intensely about her desperate need to present her case graciously despite any emotionally upsetting response from him.

Then during her prayer time God gave her two significant ideas. She had planned only to discuss her own need for in-depth communication in their marriage, yet that would just point the finger at how he'd failed. What if she changed her emphasis to the two lists of five needs that a husband and wife want from their spouse? Then the focus would be on what both of them could do to improve their marriage. Also it would give Scott a chance to express any disappointment he had with *her* as his wife as well—and she would learn what she could do about it.

Then she recalled hearing of terribly busy Christian couples who made a point of having a date night once a week. This assured them of time set aside for talk and sharing. *That could be the solution to our problem!* she thought.

Theresa also planned strategies for the possibility that Scott might begin saying harsh or hurtful things to her. She decided she'd better leave the room rather than risk blowing up at him. Perhaps she should pack her tote bag so she'd be ready to leave the house and go to a coffee shop to read for awhile, to give Scott time to cool down. But after praying about that, she realized that if she left and he didn't know where she was going, he'd probably worry. Then she saw that her real motive was to hurt him because he'd hurt her, so she cancelled the idea.

Her Christian cleaning lady came that Saturday as usual. Theresa asked if they could pray together "about an important discussion I'm planning to have with Scott this afternoon," and this short time of prayer helped calm Theresa's nerves, adding one more spiritual weapon to her arsenal.

When Scott arrived home later, he told her how he'd shoved someone who'd gotten angry at him on the subway. He'd been mystified for years as to why people were so rude to him at Grand Central Station, totally   unaware of how he violated people's private space while walking briskly to catch a train. Normally, Theresa, who could see he brought this kind of response on himself, would have silently condemned him, but today she merely smiled in an understanding way as she listened. *I'm acting like an insecure teenager, trying to make a boy like me so he'll ask me for a date,* she thought. At once she saw how afraid she felt about his possible anger during their "appointment" in a few hours.

Then Scott fell asleep on the couch. Four o'clock came and went and he slept on. *Maybe he's sleeping because he's dreading this discussion, too,* she thought.

Finally she gathered her courage and walked into the living room. He had just awakened, and to her amazement his face revealed no dread or pain as she pulled a chair up to the couch.

"What I especially wanted to talk about this afternoon is my need for conversation in our marriage," she began. "Then I thought it would be more fair if we discussed those lists of five things that both of us want from our marriage and see how we're doing."

Scott seemed totally unthreatened by this beginning. They discussed the first need on a husband's list—sexual fulfillment—and went on to the first item on the wife's list—affection. When they arrived at the topic of a wife's need for conversation, she recounted the incident when he threatened to leave her if she insisted on discussions. He had totally forgotten the episode. "Maybe I felt manipulated," he said, and he totally rejected the idea of leaving her as not being his true feeling at all.

Then she praised him for his frequent thoughtfulness—picking up a few groceries on his way home from work, fixing the plant hanger in the kitchen the day after she'd asked him to, and other such deeds.

"I often thank God for your thoughtfulness," she added, "but you seem to have a blind spot. You're good at listening to your business clients, your colleagues at work and our children, but I encounter silence when I try to share what's on my heart. You don't know any of the most exciting things happening in my life, but my girlfriends do, and this hurts. I want you to know what I'm learning; I want you to be involved in my life."

He sighed. "Well, it's this way, Theresa," he began. "When I come home from work, if you pour a stream of words over me I feel ambushed. And when my mind is absorbed trying to solve a business problem, I can't tune into anything deep that you're attempting to tell me. The business problem saps all my strength." At long last, Theresa understood his behavior.

At that point she told him about her idea for a possible solution. "I've heard of busy Christian couples who go out on a date once a week and just share with each other what they've been thinking. Could we try something like that?"

"That's a great idea," he responded. "Why don't we go out for dinner every Sunday night?"

"Oh, I like that!" said Theresa. "Let's start next week."

"Let's start tomorrow!" he countered.

Theresa could not believe her ears. The atmosphere of their entire discussion about the scary issue had been pleasant. Her hurt and resentment evaporated.

After talking about all five behaviors that husbands and wives want from each other, Theresa walked around their home in a state of awe for the next few hours. She'd witnessed God intervening in their marriage in an unbelievable and breathtaking way. Her heart could do nothing but praise Him.

For months Scott and Theresa went out to dinner regularly on Sunday night. But one week the city was struck by a ferocious snowstorm so they stayed home. Another Sunday, Scott didn't feel well, and gradually their habit of going out on Sunday nights began to wane. But now Scott started lingering after dinner to discuss whatever they'd been thinking or doing that day, often for thirty or forty-five minutes. So it didn't matter that their Sunday dates had ceased. Theresa could discuss deep issues with him on a regular basis and she felt satisfied.

One day she realized that she'd stopped daydreaming about Dave long ago. Scott was meeting her longing for meaningful conversation and she no longer was fantasizing about marrying Dave to fill her emotional vacuum.

Sometime later, Scott was watching a video by himself in the living room and called Theresa in to watch a certain scene. The movie was about a man and woman who lived together and they were arguing about their relationship. The man was basically happy with things the way they were. He'd left his wife because she was too emotionally demanding. Now the woman he lived with also wanted more involvement with him, more conversation, and again he felt crowded.

"Theresa, this is what you were talking about," Scott said. "I think there are many couples who have this problem. Maybe we should replay this segment when we have couples over for dinner and then we could have a discussion about what's going on in this scene and what it means for all our marriages."

Theresa was dumbfounded. Rather than leaving her, Scott had changed and matured in an amazing way. He now even wanted to help others in his area of weakness.

* * *

Six months after Scott and Theresa James started going out for dates on Sunday nights, the two of them went to a Christian conference where Scott was asked to give a ten-minute talk at a men's seminar. He spoke on what God had taught him about marriage. The rest of the week, men kept seeking him out, wanting his counsel.

Sometime later a group of young mothers at the James' church asked Theresa to speak to them about marriage. She shared the story about trusting God for meaningful conversation with her husband. The message they heard was: *It's OK if you can't get through to your husband about how his behavior is hurting you. God still changes lives.* She convinced them that Jeremiah's words described reality:

Behold, I am the Lord, the God of all flesh:
is there any thing too hard for me?
Jeremish 32:27 KJV

A person never really knows how far his influence extends. What husbands became better husbands after hearing Scott speak at the Christian conference? What neighbors saw those men's changed behavior toward their wives and decided to follow suit? What children in those families were affected and became better parents themselves later on? What women who heard Theresa speak clung to God's promises and courageously confronted their husbands, too? What children in those homes grew up watching a far better marriage between their parents that the little ones could chose to imitate in the future?

The ripples from one rock thrown in the water, one husband changing his attitude, just keep going on. Someday in heaven people will see how far the eternal ripples went.

Chapter Three

THE MAN
WHO WOULDN'T GIVE UP

Chemagea had spent most of the day fetching water for her family. The tin can she balanced so carefully on her head held only two gallons, and to get it, she had walked three hours to the spring and then waited in a long line for still more hours to get her chance at the life-giving flow. When she finally filled her can, she now had the three-hour trip home, watching carefully where she stepped. To trip and fall with the precious fluid would mean another long walk back and another long wait in line. She couldn't bear the thought of such a calamity.

As she stooped to enter her family's grass hut, she wanted nothing more than just to sit down and rest for a moment. To her dismay, in the shadowy interior she saw two white visitors—missionaries Art and Mary Ellen Davis. Now she had to share her meager supply of water with these unexpected guests, for no one in the Pokot tribe would ever entertain callers without offering them something to drink—tea, milk or water. And it was such a hot day! The Davises had given her husband a ride in their car as they traveled toward the village. It was just unthinkable not to treat them hospitably.

Adventurer Art Davis, 1991.

Unknown to Chemagea, her husband had almost refused the offered ride home, for he knew that nowhere in his humble hut did he have a drop of anything to drink until his wife returned from her long and dusty trek to the spring. Water is a crucial necessity anywhere and is as rare and costly as jewels to the Pokot people.

Art and Mary Ellen had been sent by the African Inland Church to study the possibility of an outreach to this animistic tribe[1] wandering over the semi-desert of northern Kenya. The tribesmen go everywhere on foot, carrying spears far longer than they are tall, in case they encounter lions as they search for water and grazing for their cattle.

---

[1]Animists believe that there are spirits in trees, rocks, and countless other inanimate objects. People must placate these spirits, or else the spirits will cause trouble. When someone gets sick, animists think that this person has angered a certain spirit, and they'll make a sacrifice, often a chicken, to the spirit so that the sick person will get well.

As Art and Mary Ellen sat in Chemagea's hut that day, Art thought, *Somehow we have to find a way to get these people water.* In that region of Kenya, no rain had fallen for over two years, and the grass needed for the cattle to graze was disappearing into the parched earth of the desert.

Soon after that when Art and Mary Ellen returned to the United States for their regular furlough, he couldn't get the Pokots out of his mind. One day he was reading the book of Isaiah and came across these words:

> *The poor and needy search for water,*
> *but there is none;*
> *their tongues are parched with thirst.*
> *But I the Lord will answer them . . . .*
> *I will turn the desert into pools of water, . . .*
> *so that people may see and know . . .*
> *that the hand of the Lord has done this.*
> Isaiah 41:17-20

"O Lord, do it!" Art cried out.

Later that day as he spoke at a conference, he told the people about Chemagea and her six-hour walk for a mere two gallons of water which she carried back to her family on her head. He read the verses from Isaiah and said, "Our burden is to take back resources to drill wells for these people." At the end of the meeting, a man in the audience came up to Art with tears in his eyes and offered to sell him a drilling rig at a discount. In the end, he charged Art less than a fifth of the original price for the equipment.

The Davises returned expectantly to Kenya to set up housekeeping in a grass hut in Orus, an area where the Pokots' grass huts were scattered sparsely about. Art and

Mary Ellen didn't want to build more permanent housing until they found out where water was located. Meanwhile, the drilling rig was making its slow and ponderous way across the ocean in a freighter and wouldn't get there for seven long months. So twice a week the Davises drove their truck fourteen miles along a rough and rocky road to get twenty gallons of water for their household. The round trip took four hours, and to make the water last as long as possible, all four members of the family would bathe with water in one bucket.

Throughout their history the Pokot people had put their trust in the spirits who, they believed, lived in the surrounding mountains and the stars overhead. They also called on the spirits of their dead ancestors to help them through life's constant problems. It didn't occur to them that Christianity held hope for them, it seemed too strange.

Every Sunday Art and Mary Ellen would hold a worship service, assisted by a Christian Pokot named Ruben. About fifty tribespeople would arrive to hear about this strange new religion that Ruben, his wife and the Davises were talking about. At the end of the service the people would linger to ask questions—lots of questions.

After a few months of attending these casual meetings, an elderly diviner stood up at the end of the service and pointed at Art. "You say you come from God. Can this God bring rain? You say you have this Jesus who can work miracles. We've done everything according to our traditions to try to get our gods to hear us and send rain, but they refuse to do it and have thrown us away."

Art stood there, astonished. Immediately he began to think, *This is impossible! What if I pray and it doesn't rain? That would make Jesus look powerless.* Then the Holy Spirit

spoke quietly to him: *Pray, and leave the results to Me.*
Besides, the man wasn't asking if Art himself could bring
rain, but if Art's God could.

"Yes, God can send rain," Art replied, "but first we must
do two things: We must repent of our sins. And we must
pray only in the name of Jesus for rain."

The Pokot tribesmen often stole cattle from the neighboring Turkana tribe and frequently killed people during
these raids. They saw nothing wrong with this and didn't
understand that such behavior affected whether Jesus
would answer their prayers or not. Art knew he needed
to communicate to them the concept of Isaiah 59:1-2—

The arm of the Lord is not too short to save,
nor his ear too dull to hear.
But . . . your sins have hidden his face from you,
so that he will not hear.

Art explained to them that stealing and killing upset God
and that they needed to tell Him they were very sorry—
and mean it.

All fifty people in the congregation agreed to Art's
requirements; they were so desperate for rain they would
have agreed to nearly anything. Then the old diviner stood
up again. "Let's also pray to our gods so they can share in
the credit if rain comes." Ruben, who'd been translating
Art's words into Pokot, didn't even wait for Art to reply.
"Absolutely not!" he exclaimed. "You told us your gods
have failed. Today we will pray only in Jesus' name!"
Everyone in the group agreed, shouting at the old man to
sit down.

Then Art prayed, declaring their repentance before God

and asking Him for rain in the name of Jesus.

All day long the sky remained sunny and as usual the majestic night canopy twinkled with billions of stars. Not a puff of a cloud was in sight. But the next day a big black cloud hovered ominously over the area as Art and Mary Ellen drove off in their truck to buy supplies in a town sixty miles away.

When they returned two days later they were astounded to feel their truck tires sliding on the muddy road. The Pokot people greeted them with huge grins. Rain had come, heavy downpours for an hour, two days in a row! The rain had knocked over the Davises' tent; all their belongings were soaked. It rained an hour a day for three more days, and each time it rained only in Orus; all the surrounding areas remained dry.

Everyone was talking about it. The next Sunday, the elderly diviner stood up in church and said, "Truly it is Jesus who has power with God." And slowly over the coming months, twelve Pokot people made a commitment to Jesus Christ.

After the long, ocean voyage, the drill rig finally arrived. But its operation was highly technical and dangerous so Art and his eager helpers were forced to wait three more months until at last two technicians showed up.

The tribesmen looked on anxiously as the newcomers proceeded to dig one well after another. After digging four of them, they finally had one that produced water, but only enough for two families. They still needed water not only for all the other households, but also for their cattle. However, the technicians had to go home and as soon as they left, the rig broke down.

Greatly discouraged, Art made the six-hour trip to the

capital city of Nairobi, where he hoped to find spare parts
for the rig. While there, he "just happened" to meet a man
who needed a job as a well-driller. Delighted, Art hired
him on the spot and brought him back to Orus. The man
dug a fifth well two miles away from the first ones, but the
drill bit and its cable got stuck in the hole. It took a month
to get them out, costing three thousand dollars. By now
the project had run out of money; the drilling was forced to
come to a stop.

This is hopeless, thought Art. *All this expense and all this
effort, yet we still have so little water.* In their gloom Art and
the other believers managed to squeak out a prayer that
God would somehow provide the badly needed water.

Then one day a few people from a mission group called
Feed the Children visited Orus. "We hear you have a well-
drilling machine. Do you need money? Can we help you
financially?" Could they help?! With great joy the
missionaries and the Pokot people accepted the gift. The
visitors contributed enough funds to dig two more wells,
so Art and his co-workers went back to the fifth well and
completed it. However, it produced so little water that it
wasn't worth pumping.

Forlorn, many of the Pokot moved on to find water and
grazing for their cattle in some other place. To keep their
cows alive, they usually needed to move four times a year
to find enough grass and water for them.

Art and the others persisted and dug a sixth well. It
produced more than three hundred gallons of water a day,
causing great excitement. But again, that wasn't enough
for the entire community plus their livestock.

Locating a good place to dig a well is a tricky business.
Fault lines run here and there throughout the area and these

cracks in the rocky crust of the earth were the most likely places to find subterranean streams. An air survey was the best way to see where the fault lines lay, but how would they find someone knowledgeable enough to do such a survey? Then a pilot came to visit his parents—Earl and Esther Anderson, missionaries who worked alongside the Davises. He was able to fly a small plane over the entire area, mapping out exactly where the fault lines ran.

As people in many parts of the world know, the presence of underground water makes a green twig bend downward. So with guidance from his pilot-son, Earl Anderson carried a y-shaped twig back and forth across the area of the fault line. The location of the previous six wells that they had dug had first been determined with Earl's green twigs. Now full of hope, they began to dig the seventh well. Suddenly they struck water, lots of water! Up it came—one hundred and fifty gallons an hour all day every day without stopping. At long last they were beginning to tap into enough water to start really helping the community.

But four days later, their joy was snuffed out by tragedy: Earl Anderson was injured in a car accident. He died a month later, having given his life to provide both physical as well as spiritual water to the Pokot people.

Art and his team went back to the first well to see if they could possibly find more water by digging deeper. While they dug, the drilling rig motor ground to a halt and nothing that anyone tried could revive it. Utterly frustrated, Art walked slowly back to his tent and told Mary Ellen, "We might as well throw this machine away. We'll never find enough water here." He was so angry that he feared he wasn't showing Christ's love to the people. *What good is*

Mary Ellen Davis with a Pokot friend.

*my labor for water if my behavior contradicts the message I've
come to bring them?* he thought.

At just about that time, six elderly tribal leaders
appeared outside the Davises' tent. "We want to talk to
you," they said. Art did not know how he could possibly
face six people and listen to their problems when he couldn't
even handle his own. Wearily he composed himself and
sat down with them as Mary Ellen extended the usual form
of Kenyan hospitality—tea.

They chatted pleasantly for five minutes and then the
men said, "We've been watching you for a year and a half."

Oh, no! thought Art, his mind suddenly racing with
memories of various times he felt he'd failed them. Like
the day his truck had been full and he hadn't stopped to
pick up one of these men. And the time he'd been so
frustrated with the well-digging that he'd spoken crossly
to another one of them when the man asked Art for a favor.
Not like Jesus at all. And worst of all, he hadn't found

them enough water.

The old men continued talking: "You've been very patient, trying to get water for us. You haven't quit. You keep trying. Please do not give up. Other white people have come to help us but have left because the land is too harsh for them. But you have persevered. You surely must have a very powerful God. We want to hear about Him."

Dumbfounded, Art sat silent. What he saw in himself was weakness and failure, especially failure to find enough water. Yet God was using Art's weakness and failure to force him to keep on looking for water, manifesting a perseverance these people needed to see.

In the days that followed, Art and Ruben relished talking with these six leaders about the Lord. However, like Pharoah,[2] they'd see God's miracles over and over and yet still they would not put their trust in Christ. That seemed to be their pattern.

One day Art's brother Ray came for a visit and managed to fix the drill rig motor, enabling them to go back to their first well and drill it one hundred feet deeper. The initial drillers hadn't brought equipment that could go down that far. To the amazement of all of them, that dry well suddenly began pumping over one thousand gallons of water an hour. Stunned, Art said, "If only we'd dug just one hundred feet farther the first time, then our problems would never have happened. But then . . . none of the blessings that have come as a result of persevering would have come our way either."

Now they had two exceptional wells. But how could they bring the water up out of the earth to take care of all

[2] See Exodus, chapters 5-11.

their needs? Their hand pumps worked well enough to provide for the people themselves, but to water hundreds of thirsty cows and goats, they needed some other source of power. With no electricity in the area, generators would be needed to run the pumps.

However, once more they'd come to the end of their money; the project came to a standstill. Again, all they could do was cry out to God to help them.

It was not long before a Canadian friend visited Art and Mary Ellen and offered aid from the Canadian government to buy two pumps and the engines to run them—a thirty-thousand-dollar gift from a totally unexpected source.

To celebrate the triumph from all this labor, the Christians in the area plus a large group of Pokot unbelievers held a dedication ceremony at the last well. A pastor from a neighboring Kenyan tribe came to speak at the dedication. He asked the Pokots, "Did any of your diviners or wise men ever tell you that there was water at this spot?"

The question took them by surprise. "No," they said in wonder. They had been in the habit of relying on their diviners to solve all their problems because they were sure these men had access to the gods.

"The elder I respected the most lived in this area for years," said one of the older men, "but he never said anything about water being right here."

The pastor replied, "This is evidence that God loves you. He loves the Pokot so much that He brought His servants here to find water for you and your cattle. These people lived far away, but they came nevertheless." The Pokot began to realize that they'd been crediting their diviners with supernatural insight that they obviously didn't have.

These hard-working foreigners really did have a God worth worshiping.

Before the Davises had come to live there two years before, all that the Pokot knew about Christianity was that some odd, religious people would meet regularly in a place called a church. They wanted no part of this strange group.

Now that the Pokot saw that the Christian God was worth knowing, their well-known resistance to change stood in the way. In the end no one person or event finally convinced the tribespeople to trust in Christ—not the prayed-for rain, not the perseverance of the missionaries, not even flowing water from the wells. "Tribes of herders will watch you and your message for a long time," Bishop Ezekiel Birech told Art. "And then there will be a change."

In 1991, seven years after the Davises first set their hearts on bringing water to the Pokot, there were just fifty baptized believers in the area. Resistance to change and to the Gospel itself remained constant and fierce. It took God's work in a nineteen-year-old boy to accelerate their response to Christ's love.

Five thousand miles away in Tumbridge Wells, England, Peter Jackson wanted to spend the summer in Kenya before going to university. He was a hiker and an explorer, and assisting the Davises in their mission seemed the right step before beginning the demanding work of university

Nineteen-year-old Pete Jackson.

studies. He flew to Kenya for the summer and Art quickly came to appreciate the deep godliness and faith of this young man. Soon he was overseeing the development and spiritual work of four churches, serving five thousand Pokot. "He did a splendid job," says Art. "He endeared himself to the people, serving them day and night. He loved it here."

Early one morning some men from the enemy Turkana tribe came to steal cows from the corral of one of the Pokot Christians who regularly went out to preach the Gospel. Peter was guarding the cows while the owner was gone.

The Turkanas broke open the door of Peter's round tin hut near the corral and questioned him. *How could he be telling the truth, saying he's unarmed, if he's protecting these cows?* they thought. High on a local drug called *miraa*, the thieves shot him four times in the chest at point-blank range. He died instantly.

A young Pokot herdsman had been nearby and overheard the conversation and the shots. Quietly he crept away to escape and told people what had happened. When Peter's British friends received word of the tragedy, they committed themselves to pray fervently for the Pokot and the Turkana so that Peter would not have died in vain. Their prayers became a mighty force that produced a great response to the Gospel.

Since then, ten Turkana and ten Pokot have attended Bible school, financed by the Peter Jackson Memorial Fund. And these ten Turkana have already led dozens of their fellow tribesmen to the Lord. In addition, every month twelve Pokot believers fly by helicopter, supplied by a Swiss mission, to tell their people in remote villages about Jesus Christ. Each of these outings lasts four days.

By 2001, the Body of Christ in the Pokot tribe had mushroomed to over two thousand believers in forty churches. Half of those churches grew up as a result of the struggling beginnings of the Davises and their coworkers. They've been working to provide enough water for the Pokot now for nineteen years and are still plodding onward.

The water, however, has not been the primary vehicle for impact. Concerted prayer around the world has provided the spiritual dynamite needed to beat down the forces of darkness. And the Christian message has drawn people because it was backed by powerful acts of God and godly lives. "Jesus brought more than a message," says Art. "He healed and did miracles. And that gave weight to what He said."

* * *

Art and Mary Ellen Davis have been living for decades in a hot and arid place which no one would describe as beautiful. They have no electricity, no air-conditioning, no paved roads, no UPS, no telephone, no computer, no e-mail, no videos, no shopping malls. They took upon themselves a task that appeared insurmountable. Can the Davises really say today that it's been worth it?

A missionary's greatest joy comes when people living in darkness realize at last that Jesus wants to bring His light to dispel their oppressing situation. Crippling pagan beliefs plus life-threatening physical circumstances have held the Pokot people in bondage for millenia. Yet Art and Mary Ellen have seen God use them—two weak, human vessels—to establish a major beachhead for the Gospel in what was once Satan's domain.

In the meantime the Lord has etched the image of His Son deeply into the Davises through the countless obstacles they have had to overcome. These two people have had to rely totally on God for grace to keep right on trying to find water, to care for the Pokot people's welfare so much that they refused to give in to normal human discouragement. And in the process, more and more of Jesus came to be seen in them. That's exactly what the Pokot needed to see clearly—Jesus, who could flood their lives with His light. The Davises became more beautiful people, God received greater and greater glory from their lives, and needy people actually observed what Jesus is really like.

But what about Peter Jackson? His life was abruptly cut short. Back in England his parents' great grief, in time, found comfort in this: Their son's spilt blood so mobilized a mighty wave of prayer that the people in the tribe of his killers were repenting and going to Bible school to learn to spread the Light in their own communities. Did not Peter go to Kenya for this very reason? He would have been ecstatic to see such a result from his short stay in East Africa.

Jesus knew the secret to getting such spectacular results:

I tell you the truth,
unless a kernel of wheat falls to the ground and dies,
it remains only a single seed.
But if it dies,
it produces many seeds.
John 12:24

So God, without Peter's permission or foreknowledge, turned this young man's life into the ground; now countless Pokot and Turkana seeds are being produced because of the fertilizer of one life.

Peter didn't really think that he would pay such a high

price nor did he expect such an extraordinary harvest from his time in Kenya. It would be phenomenal to see that much fruit after a half century of living. But God chose to compress Peter's ministry and its eternal results into a short time span.

The fruit of Peter's time in Kenya will one day walk into heaven and personally thank him for risking his life so that they could find freedom from darkness. As he shakes each of their hands there, what word in earth's vocabulary is adequate to describe the level of joy and gratitude he will feel? There is no such word.

Peter Jackson and Art and Mary Ellen Davis consider the price they've paid in Kenya a minor issue; they see only the richness that God has given as a result of their lives spent in a primitive area. They view themselves as extraordinarily fortunate to have been used by God to such a degree.

Chapter Four

DESTINATION UNKNOWN

Sophie had a problem. She'd been a Christian for a very short time and now she discovered she was pregnant. Even though she still loved him, she had ended her affair with Mutiso the day she gave her life to Christ.

But now, how could she go to church with her pregnancy becoming more and more apparent each week? She decided that her best option was to avoid attending the worship services until her baby was born. But her close friend Sarah did not agree. "That's stupid!" she said. Sarah had prayed for Sophie's conversion for twelve years, ever since they'd played together in grade school. So Sophie Akatsa swallowed her pride and went to church. Her daughter Charmaine was born some months later.

Mutiso badly wanted to marry Sophie. But not only did he not walk with God, he was not even a Christian, so

Sophie knew she couldn't marry him. The Scriptures were growing increasingly precious to her and she was aware of what it said about marriage for believers:

Do not be yoked together
with unbelievers.
For what do righteousness and wickedness
have in common?
2 Corinthians 6:14

So, although she couldn't marry him, she began praying intensely for Mutiso to come to a place where he would want to commit his life to Christ.

In the African tradition, if a woman becomes pregnant she marries her lover. However, if they don't marry, he must give two cows to her family and then the child belongs to the father and his relatives. However, Sophie wouldn't accept any such gift from Mutiso's family. She wanted to raise Charmaine herself and teach her to love the Lord.

As time passed, other men became drawn to Sophie and wanted to marry her. Her vivacious personality made her seem so alive, so appealing. But she couldn't stop longing for Mutiso and each year she prayed more intensely for him to turn to Christ. Occasionally he would contact her and she kept his photo in a frame in her house. Time and again she'd tell Charmaine, "This is your father."

After his affair with Sophie, Mutiso fathered a son by another woman who wanted to marry him. "I'm sorry," he told her, "I love Sophie." So the woman gave her son to Mutiso's family and married someone else.

One night Sophie and her girlfriend joined two hundred

and fifty other Christians at an all-night prayer meeting at their church. Half way through the night the two women fervently asked God to send them both husbands. Soon after that, Mutiso appeared at Sophie's gate. When she came out to see him, he asked her point-blank, "What are the conditions under which you'd be willing to marry me?"

She immediately showed him the Bible verse about believers not being yoked with unbelievers. He seemed interested in giving his life to the Lord, and she suggested that he go to see the distinguished chaplain who served at the boarding school that Mutiso had attended. He did so right away, but still didn't turn his life over to Christ. For four more years Sophie prayed even more intensely for Mutiso to put his trust in Jesus so that they could be married and have a family.

Then one day he was assaulted in a bar. He struggled home and died of internal bleeding two days later, alone in his house. He was twenty-eight years old.

Sophie received a call late that night, telling her that Mutiso was dead. She was devastated. *Why pray?* she thought. *I prayed for so long, and God didn't answer. So what's the use of praying at all?*

Day after day she couldn't sleep or eat. At night she felt a burning sensation deep inside her calves, but doctors could find nothing wrong with her. *I won't ask God for anything ever again,* she thought, *because what's the use? He'll just do what He wants to do anyway.* She'd worship God at church, thank Him, and confess her sins. But she quit asking Him for anything.

"I'd die if I couldn't ask God for anything," her friend protested. And that was exactly what was happening to Sophie. The life was draining out of her as she lived each day without food or sleep.

When a person passes away in Kenya, friends and relatives come and live in the house of the dead person to comfort the family. But in Sophie's case, people didn't know how deep her emotional involvement with Mutiso had been. Therefore, no one commiserated with her and she suffered alone. She'd go to bed with the lights on in her room because she feared that his ghost might come to her in the darkness.

Then one day at work when her boss was out, Sophie lay down prostrate on the floor of his office, broken before God: "Lord, please forgive me for my pride. Who am I, the pot, to tell the Potter what to do? You are in control and You know what is best." She cried out to God to give her back her life. She asked Him for an appetite and the ability to sleep. It was the first time she'd asked God for anything in six months.

Furthermore, Sophie was also deeply burdened about whether Mutiso was in heaven or hell.[1] Then a wise Christian woman whom Sophie hardly knew suggested, "Why don't you ask God to show you where Mutiso is?" Sophie had considered that. However it would shatter her if she were to learn that he'd gone to hell.

Then she remembered what had happened to her Canadian pastor's wife: Their grown son had gone sledding in Canada's snow and hit a pole. He was electrocuted. He then became like a vegetable, kept alive only by machines. The family prayed, "O Lord! Would You please take him?" And as soon as they said, "Amen," he died. The mother didn't know if her son had gone to heaven or hell. He had put his trust in Christ at one point in his life, but later he'd

[1] See Appendix A to understand how a person can be sure.

quit walking with God. She asked God to show her and the Lord spoke to her heart, *You have no idea of the depths of My mercy and My love.*

Recalling this, Sophie thought, *Should I ask God to show me?* But she couldn't get past her fear that Mutiso might be in hell. Then she thought about her relationship with her daughter and this helped her see how her heavenly Father would treat her: If Charmaine asked Sophie a question, she wouldn't give her daughter an answer that would shatter her. *Besides, why would God put it in my heart to ask Him this if the answer would devastate me?* she reasoned. In fact, the prophet Isaiah foretold that the coming Messiah would act just as Sophie thought He would:

A bruised reed he will not break
and a smoldering wick he will not snuff out.
Isaiah 42:3

So she asked God to show her if Mutiso were in heaven or hell. Two nights later she dozed off and had a dream. She saw Mutiso smiling at her and woke up with a jerk. *What does this mean?* she wondered. *Is he in heaven?* Then she had another dream: The phone call came, announcing his death. She went to his funeral in the rural area where his relatives lived. Everyone wore white. Mutiso walked in and sat on a bench beside her. "Sophie," he said, "the night before I died, I made my peace with God."

She woke up from this dream with a heart at peace. The issue was settled. Now she could sleep. Now she could eat. Excitedly she told his brothers and sisters, "Mutiso is in heaven! God showed me!" Puzzled, they stared at her. Not being Christians, they didn't comprehend at all. Then

Mutiso's family wanted to give Sophie some of the inherit-
ance for Charmaine. Sophie thought, *Are they trying to gain
control over her?* Troubled by this thought, she refused. She
had not even taken Charmaine, now five years old, to the
funeral, for fear that the family would try to claim her as
their own.

Soon it was Christmas, and Sophie took Charmaine to
spend the holidays with her parents in the rural area where
they lived. While they were there her father began to talk
about Sophie's life. In the soft light of their kerosene lan-
terns he strode back and forth, shouting at her, "Charmaine
belongs to Mutiso's family!" He'd been suppressing his
emotions all these years over how Sophie was violating their
tribal traditions: A child belongs to the father.

Many people thought that Sophie should have married
Mutiso, and both her family and his blamed her for his
death. If she had married him, he would not have been out
at that bar that night, they all said. Sophie was crushed.
Now she realized that her father didn't want her child, and
she herself had refused to let Mutiso's family claim her. So
if Sophie should suddenly die, Charmaine would belong
to no one and would have no family at all. This idea
troubled her deeply and she kept trying to figure out what
to do about it.

Soon Sophie started showing up at parties thrown by
Mutiso's family, even though she hadn't been invited.
Every time she came, she brought them gifts. She learned
about some of the family's struggles: Mutiso's brother had
a drinking problem, and his wife became so depressed
about it that she had to spend several months in a hospital.
Sophie reached out to their three children, and they grew
to love being with her. She even led one of them to the

Lord. She also visited the brother's wife in the hospital and led her to Christ. To everyone's amazement, the wife recovered and no longer needed the medication that the psychiatrist had prescribed for her.

Mutiso's mother had become blind due to a stroke. She became fond of Sophie and looked forward to her visits. Whenever Sophie arrived, the mother wanted her to

Sophie Akatsa and Charmaine in 1991.

share her bed with her, a special honor, and Sophie became more and more a member of their family.

Now Sophie lives at peace, for Charmaine has a family, Mutiso is at home in heaven, and his relatives are becoming Christians.

* * *

When Sophie was going through torment for months, she had no idea how significant would be the rewards of this time of severe testing in her life:

All the great saints in the Bible had God personally reveal truth to them that otherwise could not have been known. This one Kenyan woman in the twentieth century joined their august ranks as one of those to whom God personally reveals what He alone knows.

Many times Christian women compromise biblical standards when they fall in love with a non-Christian and marry him. God's wisdom is often revealed in their later pain. Yet here was a woman who chose, against her will, to live by God's standard and even suffer for it. The news of her choice spread everywhere that Mutiso's family and friends lived. It's one thing to hear about God's standard, but another thing to know someone who actually lives by it. Thus, Sophie's decision became a forceful example to other believers.

Every Christian parent longs for her child to learn unequivocably how wonderful God is. Imbedded in the history of Charmaine's short life are such mighty acts of God that she can't shake Him off; His greatness is too much a part of her background and personhood.

Climactically, Mutiso's death propelled Sophie into relationship with his relatives. They saw her life; they felt her love; they relished her vivacious personality. And one by one they've been coming to know and love her God.

How could so much pain bring such astounding benefits? The only explanation is found in one of David's prayers:

You are great and do marvelous deeds;
you alone are God.

Psalm 86:10

Chapter Five

TYCOON INTERRUPTED

Pete McDonald didn't look like a failure. Recently he'd sold his own company, an enterprise he'd developed from the ground up by his own hard work over a period of thirteen years. He'd now become president of a subsidiary of the corporation that had purchased his firm. But two weeks into his new position he was suddenly demoted, and within a month he was without a job of any kind.

That day will burn in his memory forever. Pete is a warrior and he wanted vengeance. The corporation had promised him a future; they'd promised him millions of dollars. Instead he received two months' salary. He was president of the new company for only two weeks and with his signed contracts he had a strong case for legal action.

His employees didn't like the way the corporation executives had treated Pete by not honoring what they'd promised him. Not wanting to be part of such a corporation, these men also resigned within four months of Pete's departure.

At a loss, Pete flipped open the Bible study *Experiencing God* by Henry Blackaby because God had used it in such a big way in his life in the past. He turned back to it now, but not without trepidation, for it seemed that every time he spent time in this study some huge change would occur in his life. He prayed for guidance about whether to sue the corporation; his lawyer had studied the documents drawn up when Pete[1] sold his company, and the attorney felt Pete had a strong case. But first he waited to see what he would hear from God.

As Pete prayed and read the Scriptures, he turned to the account of King Saul tirelessly pursuing David in order to kill him. At one point the king had gone into a cave to relieve himself, and unknown to him, David and his men were hiding in that very cave. His soldiers urged David to sneak up on Saul and kill him, but David crept up unnoticed and cut off a corner of Saul's kingly robe instead. Later David showed the fragment to Saul to prove that he didn't harbor ill intent toward the king.

Through this story God spoke to Pete's heart to take the godly path as David had done, not demanding justice for what had happened to him, but letting the Lord resolve the situation. *God allowed this debacle to happen,* Pete thought. *Whatever God intends, He intends it for my good.* He left the situation in the Lord's hands and prayed with his wife Karen, *Lord, You are sovereign. You will reveal Your plan for me soon. If our former ideas were awesome, what You have for us now will be even better.*

---

[1] The names in this chapter have been changed.

Surely God would be as good as He had been to Pete before the corporation had bought his company outright. He thought back to those days, less than a month before, when he was running his own firm. He had loved it, working from early morning until late at night. Although it had left little time for his wife and children, he had figured that God had provided this opportunity and that things would work out. "Everything was go-go-go," he says. "I didn't want the company to fail for lack of work or dedication. I was out to change the world. I wanted to make my God and my family proud."

As a result, his firm had experienced astronomical growth. Now all that was gone, swallowed up by the ego of a billionaire, the founder of the corporation. "You're bringing in Pete to run this new company?" he'd chided the CEO of the subsidiary that Pete had become president of. "He's only thirty-five, you know. You should be able to handle this job yourself. If you can't, then you're not what you say you are."

So on the day that Pete picked up his first paycheck, the CEO had told him, "We can't have a chief executive officer as well as a president for the new company. It doesn't work for the shareholders. And it doesn't work for the bookkeeping. You can continue working for the company, but you can't be president." Pete had felt completely blindsided. He could see that he and the CEO would be trying to take the company in two different directions. *My dreams can't be realized*, Pete had thought. *I am a lame duck. I can't do what excites me. My bridges are burnt all around me.* So he had resigned.

But there was no use dwelling on the past now. So Pete hired a recruitment firm to find him a job. The recruiter was impressed. "A man with your experience and qualifications should be hired within the next four to eight weeks," he told Pete. "You've been underpaid and will most likely make twice as much money as before."

Pete had always thought he could do things better and faster than others could. *Since it usually takes about six months for normal people to find a new job,* he thought, *it should take me three months, tops. The agency will surely find me a job quickly, for I know God will provide one.*

Soon a number of interviews materialized. "You're just the kind of person we're looking for," they'd say. Time after time Pete became the top candidate for an attractive position. But later the company would tell the recruiter they were concerned that Pete would try to take over the company. His energy and entrepreneurial skills had become a threat, and in the end they would tell him, "Sorry, you're overqualified for the job."

Pete was confused. He'd always felt needed and sought out. Before his company had merged with the corporation, he would come out of church and find seven messages waiting for him on his cell phone. He sometimes logged in over forty hours a month on that phone. He'd receive calls from Canada and Ireland at nine thirty at night. "I was greatly needed," he says. "Now suddenly no one called me. There was an earthshattering silence."

A short time later, a prominent, well-known corporation became interested in Pete and flew him to three different cities so that fourteen of their top executives could interview him to become one of their vice presidents. Each one told him that he had great interviews. *This is more like it,* Pete thought. *This is fun. Finally.*

Their number-three executive said, "Pete, expect an

offer. You're the kind of man we want!" However, the leaders of the company kept arguing about bringing in someone from outside at such a high level in the corporation and could not resolve the issue among themselves. Finally, they ended up turning Pete down simply because they couldn't agree on what to do.

Four months had now elapsed since he'd resigned from the corporation that had absorbed his company. He hadn't had one bad interview since and the recruitment firm could find no fault with how he was presenting himself to the various firms. Over and over as he talked with yet another company, everything would seem favorable and positive. Discussions would go to the next level and then to the next, but just when Pete's hopes were building, he'd be rejected. He came to expect rebuff. To someone accustomed to success, this became the hardest part of the experience.

After losing this latest attractive position, Pete began to think, *What's wrong with me? What am I not doing right?* He became angry with God. Pete remembered the first days when he and the twenty-five employees in his company had jumped on board with the corporation. "We had a good business plan, great people and a lot of excitement," he says. "We were sure it would become a hundred-million-dollar company. That was our dream."

At that time Pete had felt like God was blessing him beyond his wildest expectations. Here, not even forty years old, he would be making a huge amount of money. The businessmen in the parent corporation drove Ferraris, flew private jets and owned homes around the world. "You will be the most successful and wealthiest men in our city," they had told Pete and his colleagues. Because highly successful men had spoken these words, Pete had believed them.

"The opportunity was so large," he says. "We were walking on air." He had thought, *Life is amazing. This is a dream come true. I can run my own company. In this position I can fully use all my abilities and develop a company that my children can some day become a part of.*

But now that all seemed like the distant past. *Lord, You did this great thing for me before,* Pete sighed. *Then You took it away and I thought You'd give me something even better.* Lonely, he let self-doubt creep in. After four months of job-hunting, he hadn't made any more progress than he'd made on the very first day of his search.

The Lord then spoke to his heart: *Pete, what's going on here is not about you, about your timing, or about the approval of men.* He then realized that his anger stemmed from his lack of control over the situation. *How can I make great paintings when God keeps taking away my brushes?* he thought.

Occasionally throughout his life he'd been aware of his own smallness as compared to God's greatness, but never so starkly as now. He realized, *I'm here for God's purposes and His agenda. He's a jealous God and I'm to serve an audience of One.* Meanwhile, he was reading the Scriptures every day for an hour. Psalm 50 reminded him to praise God for who He is, regardless of what Pete was or was not. Then an old familiar verse riveted him with its contrast to the way he'd been living:

> *I can do all things*
> *through Him who strengthens me.*
> Philippians 4:13 NASB

He realized, *All my efforts, talents and pursuits are absolutely nothing without the Lord, but are everything with Him.* His new awareness of how he'd been trusting in his own efforts startled him.

He began to pray more than he ever had before. He read books. He listened to worship songs. Pete and Karen found that these activities were reprogramming their thinking. But some days his efforts seemed so futile that he didn't even feel like getting out of bed. Pete was just sick and tired of telling people that things were OK when they weren't. He began to understand how Job felt, and the cry of his heart was just like Job's:

Why did I not die at birth?
Job 3:11 RSV

God gently reminded Pete through Psalm 139 that He knew every detail of his life. As he pored over that chapter, liberating light pierced his gloom: *God has orchestrated everything. I am not the painter, but a miniscule dab of paint on His magnificant masterpiece. In spite of this situation that seems void of God's presence, He IS here.*

Pete realized that God couldn't have gotten his and Karen's attention without bringing him to the lowest point he'd ever experienced. With three children, no money, no job prospects, and even the loss of his ego, he felt utterly inadequate for the first time in his life. Just like the great men in the Scriptures, Pete cried out, *O God, I am nothing. I can't accomplish anything without You.*

Within three months the McDonalds had spent all their investments except the money locked up in their retirement accounts. Karen, a conscientious, stay-at-home mother, cared for their three children, ages one, four and five, while carefully deciding where each penny went. She and Pete would wake up in the morning with no idea where the money would come from to buy groceries that day.

But to their amazement, an incredible influx of food and money began to pour in. The stress lifted as Pete and Karen watched God take care of them: Friends would bring them food. One day, they received a check for five hundred dollars . . . then still another for a thousand. Someone covered their mortgage payment while others paid the preschool tuition for the McDonalds' children. A college roommate whom Pete hadn't seen in four years sent them a check for ten thousand dollars, with a note that said, "This is a loan if you can pay it back, a gift if you can't."

Both Pete and Karen had been missionary kids. When he was thirteen, his uncle had asked him, "Do you want to be a missionary like your dad when you grow up?"

"No, I want to support missionaries like my dad," he'd replied. But now missionaries whom Pete and Karen had supported were the first to send money to the McDonalds. It was humbling.

Pete cancelled the contract with the recruiting firm whom he'd paid several thousand dollars for their services. They'd promised to find him a job in four to eight weeks, but five months had now elapsed with no position in sight.

When Pete had first resigned from the huge corporation, he and Karen had listed nine items that they wanted in his next job. Praying over each criterion, they evaluated every one of Pete's job opportunities in light of this list. First, they would prefer to live in Virginia where both sets of parents lived, but all the possible jobs to date would have required a move to other parts of the country.

Suddenly one day a company in Virginia, with which Pete had interviewed three months before, called him unexpectedly. At the time of his interview they had had no openings, but now they wanted to see him again. Less than a week later, they offered him a job as national sales manager for their corporation.

This new job included eight of the nine items on the McDonalds' wish list. The one missing item? Pete would not have an influential leadership role in this new position. Only two people would work under him, and Pete would be responsible to develop his job so that one day he would supervise eighteen to thirty employees. Though not glamorous, this post entailed everything he loved doing—developing resources, responsibilities and people. Six months and fifty-nine interviews after his search began, Pete McDonald at last had a job.

By now he'd undergone a metamorphosis. For the first time in his life, he wasn't filled with a drive to be Number One. He didn't need to run the organization he was a part of, nor did he want to influence decisions at the highest level.

Previously Pete's friends would have described him as a dedicated family man. But the stress of work always preoccupied him so deeply that his family rarely had his full attention when he was at home. Since he now no longer lived with the pressure of running an organization he rarely brought work home. The change impacted his whole family. Most notably, his children became much more secure and affectionate as his relationship with them deepened.

Pete also began relating to other people differently. He had always been intuitive and insightful into others' hurts, needs and unspoken thoughts. Now he began to use this gift of intuition in a more compassionate way, rather than just for his own gain or that of his corporation. For the first time, he began empathizing with the leaders over him, rather than criticizing them, and he better understood the choices they had to make and why.

Before his six months of unemployment, Pete had often been judgmental of the ways people under him used their gifts. "But now I see these people as fellow runners in the great marathon of life," he says. It changed the way he treated them: They soon found him warm and helpful rather than rigid and demanding.

Previously, Pete and Karen had seemed like the perfect couple to many people: He's tall and good-looking. She's an attractive, vivacious blond. They have three darling children. They both lead stimulating Bible studies. Things always seemed to go well for them. They're often asked to be the leaders of whatever they're involved in. People put them on a pedestal.

However, others now watched the McDonalds go through this humbling trial. As it broke them, it put them on the level of the folks next door. "We didn't come out of this process looking like beautiful butterflies," says Pete. Acquaintances started telling him and his wife about their problems, sicknesses, marital struggles, financial difficulties. They'd known some of these people for years and didn't realize what they struggled with. "Apparently, they felt we couldn't relate to their battles," says Pete. "But now we've become approachable. They see that we, too, are struggling in life's journey."

Before Pete's world fell apart, he used to think, *I can change the world. Let me accomplish all these great things for You, God. Just You watch how I'll use all the talents You've given me.* He saw himself as someone who could help leaders lead, as a man who could enable people and corporations to realize their full potential. This had been his life vision, despite its arrogance. "But I'm no longer driven to accomplish my agenda," he says. "I want to aim first to do what God wants me to do."

He has come to appreciate just becoming faithful in the small things of life, of having a chance to develop his own character, of being able to serve others with his God-given talents. He used to be very concerned about his calling and how well he was progressing in it. However, now he considers the most important measurements of his life to be his pursuit of Christ, fruitfulness, and faithfulness to the Lord wherever He places him each day. "Right now God wants me to just love Him and love my family," Pete says. "I'm absolutely at peace if I never again get to run anything else in my life."

A year after the experience, he could look back and conclude that he and Karen had been just too focused on themselves and what they could accomplish for God. "When a person lives in a state of survival, of being overly busy, of ever-increasing, self-imposed standards and expectations," Pete says, "it's easy to lose focus on what's important and to miss what's happening in one's family, and in one's relationship with God."

As Pete has escaped continual pursuit of accomplishment, he sees the people around him with new eyes, those who are focused solely on achievement and success. "There's more to life than personal achievement," he says.

* * *

A man's self-esteem can be so wrapped up in his career that the thought of losing his employment for a long period of time is an unthinkable nightmare. Yet after such a trial Pete McDonald came out radically richer in every area of his life.

All his values were overhauled: Whereas before he saw himself as greatly gifted to do wonders in the business world, he now sees himself as unable to accomplish anything on his own, but everything with the Lord. He exchanged arrogance for humility, which placed him in a position to be deluged with God's grace:

> *God opposes the proud*
> *but gives grace to the humble.*
> 1 Peter 5:5

If God had left him alone to continue succeeding, unhindered, the progression of his arrogance would have called forth God's increasing opposition.

In addition, Pete's view of work and success looks far different today. He still has the same unique gifts that God has given him. But he's not driven to display them, he's not driven to be Number One. He can relax and enjoy life.

All Pete's relationships also have been affected for good:

His relationship with God has acquired new depth. Now he often talks to the Lord about whatever he's doing. He views faithfulness to obey God in the simply things of life far more important than logging in forty hours of business phone calls a month.

His family life has experienced a major transformation. His wife and children know they have his attention, for mentally Pete is not at work when his family wants to relate to him. He won't come to the end of his life regretting that he didn't spend more time with his children. He can enjoy them now; he can contribute godly values to their lives while they're impressionable.

Also, Pete's relationship with his peers moved in an unexpected direction as they began to view him as a fellow-struggler in life. He gained the richness of having friends who confide in him their fears and trials, resulting in a refreshing closeness as Pete shares his struggles as well.

Even his relationship with his enemies was affected. He chose to trust God to deal with the leaders of the corporation who reneged on their promises. Surely, this won't be the last time Pete receives a severe blow from others, but now he knows how to handle it and walk away free of bitterness.

Although it appeared that Pete's CEO in the corporation brought all this upheaval into the McDonalds' lives, God Himself takes credit for it:

> *The crucible for silver and the furnace for gold,*
> *but the Lord tests hearts.*
> Proverbs 17:3

So after only six months in God's furnace Pete emerged a totally different man—more godly, more peaceful and more pleasant to have as a husband, father and friend.

Pete had expected at this point in his life to be incredibly wealthy. And that's exactly what happened, but in a far different way than he ever imagined.

Chapter Six

THE PERFECT HUSBAND

Gary Barber burst through the door, invigorated as he always was by a successful business trip. Words poured out of him as he described to his wife his latest triumphs in sales; he'd just been awarded a prize for recording one of the largest orders in the history of his company. Who wouldn't be excited? As he paused to catch his breath, he heard a stony voice say, "I don't love you anymore."

"What?!" Gary asked in shock.

"Well, maybe I still love you deep down inside," Georgia said wearily, "but I no longer feel any love for you. I don't want to be around you. We can stay together, live under the same roof, and have sort of a business relationship. But our marriage is dead as far as I'm concerned."

Gary was stunned. "What are you talking about?" he

asked in bewilderment. He knew that early in their marriage, Georgia[1] had thought that he was the greatest thing in the world. Now for a year or two, she'd been growing more and more miserable being married to him and he hadn't known a thing about it.

In contrast, Gary thought he had a good life. He'd go away on a business trip for four days a week. Then on weekends he'd play with the kids, take his wife out to dinner, sleep late on Saturday morning, play with his model airplanes, work out at the gym, watch football on TV, and go to church. After a day in the office on Monday, he'd be off on another trip. Who wouldn't think this was the perfect life?

Georgia felt a strong bond with their dog, Bumps. He lay all day in their son Jay's bedroom, and just before Jay came home from school, Bumps would go to the front door and wait. Jay would walk in, pat Bumps, take him for a walk. Then the dog would go back to the bedroom and lie down while Jay ignored him for the rest of the evening.

Georgia felt as if she were just a part of her husband's routine, like Bumps was a part of Jay's. She and Gary were just going through the motions of marriage and it seemed obvious to her that she didn't have her husband's heart.

"Furthermore," Georgia continued in her utterly honest revelation, "there won't be any lovemaking until we get this figured out. It seems that you just get caught up in the experience of sex and forget that I'm even there."

In the coming weeks the two of them continued to discuss the issue off and on. Gary used his manly approach to deal with the situation: He would look for the problem and when it was clearly defined he'd solve it, or think he had. For every concern that Georgia brought up, he'd have

---

[1] The names in this chapter have been changed.

an answer and could refute any of her arguments. Finally one day he realized that although he was winning these verbal battles, he had lost the war with his wife.

Shortly before this conflict, they had both read a book about marriage called *If Only He Knew* by Gary Smalley. Gary Barber now read and re-read this book, trying to figure out what was bothering his wife. He was totally baffled because he was sure he was a pretty good husband and could see nothing in his life that would do such damage to his relationship with Georgia.

As the impasse continued, they decided to seek counseling. Gary wanted them to meet with a woman counselor because hopefully she could explain to him how his wife thought and felt.

One day his great self-confidence was shattered. During their third session, the counselor asked Georgia, "What are Gary's priorities?"

"Well," she began, "there's his job, his hobbies, his workouts at the gym, the children. And then there's me."

Georgia could not have startled her husband more if she'd suddenly dumped a bucket of ice water on him. *She's right*, he thought in dismay. *This is my wife. She's supposed to be the most important person in my life.* He recalled the main point in Smalley's book: If a woman knows that she doesn't have first place in her husband's heart, the couple will not have a good marriage. However, when she does feel she's number one with him, the man has freedom to pursue his individual interests without objections. But as long as she knows she's not first,[2] the marriage is not going

---

[2] Some might argue that the Lord should be first in a man's heart and his wife second. "The wife is not in competition with God for a man's affections," explains Gary Barber. "I have never ever heard a man say, 'I love my wife more than I love God.' That's not the problem."

to be healthy.

After absorbing this appalling information about himself, Gary began trying to cater to Georgia's desires before he did things for himself. "Give me a list of things you want me to do around the house," he'd say. Changing the way he'd been operating most of his life was excruciating. And to his amazement, she was taking so long to respond to all his good intentions.

"Gary did so many of the right things," Georgia said later. "But I still didn't have his heart." She figured he was just doing household repairs to get what he wanted—sex.

One day as Gary sat on the sofa facing their front door, Georgia walked down the hall toward him. "I'm still not happy with our marriage," she commented. In total frustration, Gary had only one desire—to stand up, walk straight out the door, move to an apartment, and declare their marriage over. But he paused and glanced at their two children playing on the floor in front of him. He looked at the front door, his escape hatch, and thought, *This is a package deal. My kids and my wife go together, and I can't just bail out. I have to stay here and work this through. Eventually it can be good. I really think so.*

Gary and Georgia knew another Christian couple that had been going through the same struggles, except they were six months further down the road than the Barbers were. Several times they invited the other couple over and for two or three hours Gary and Georgia would lay their garbage out on the table. The other couple would explain what they'd done in that particular predicament that had made a positive difference. Being able to talk about almost anything with these friends and feeling totally safe with them really helped Gary and Georgia think through many issues in their relationship.

Another factor in their marital struggles was Gary's temptation to read pornographic magazines . . . not often, but usually once every two or three months. A strong desire would come upon him inexplicably out of the blue and he could not control it. He'd fight the impulse with all his strength and occasionally he'd win. But usually the compulsion would overcome him and he'd have to go find satisfaction in his illicit pastime. Such a compelling impulse made no sense to him, for he regularly led Bible studies and prayer meetings, and otherwise lived the life of a committed Christian.

Then one day he told Georgia about the problem. That reminded her of the day they'd driven past a certain landmark. He'd turned to her and said, "When I'm driving home from a business trip, as I pass this point I remind myself that you won't want to make love when I get home." She thought, *If I made love every day . . . if I lost that last five pounds . . . if I were really sexy in bed . . . he wouldn't have this problem with pornography. I'm horrible. It's all my fault.*

Georgia had grown up in a family that felt uncomfortable with their bodies, with physical contact, and with expressing affection. Her grandmother couldn't even say the word *bathroom*. As a result, Georgia had entered into marriage with a feeling of shame about herself physically. Now Gary's confession confirmed what she'd believed about herself all along. She didn't know that she was competing with his fantasy world of women with perfect bodies and that she therefore couldn't satisfy him. She just figured that this was something that men did. *Besides,* she thought, *a good Christian wife doesn't complain.*

Many times as Gary drove down the road, going on a

sales trip, he would remember Romans 6:14—

Sin shall not be your master.

He'd ask himself, *How can this be? How can the Holy Spirit live in me while something like this has free reign and takes over whenever it feels like it?* He couldn't figure out what to do about it and struggled and fought long and hard.

Finally he gave up. *I'll never get over this desire to look at girly pictures,* he thought. *The only way I can survive is to make a little detour every once in a while and satisfy the urge. Otherwise I'll try to live a godly life.* The whole idea disturbed and frustrated him.

Three months after Georgia had declared their marriage dead, she experienced a significant personal triumph. Together with a few friends, she was praying about her depression, anger and resentment. During that time God revealed to her that she was harboring anger and resentment toward Gary. He'd be gone four or five days a week, leaving her to look after the children, the house and the garden while also working as a school nurse. She thought, *All men are jerks who won't take care of their women.*

In addition, the Lord showed her that she was like Houdini, the magician famous for quickly getting free when locked up or bound securely. She saw herself tied up with chains at the bottom of a lake; the chains were her *shoulds.* Like:

• A good Christian *should* be engaged in that activity.
• A good Christian *should* spend her money for this cause.

What is the root of these 'shoulds'? she asked herself. *What's the truth? What's the lie?* One by one she examined her *should*s before the Lord, looking at them honestly in the light of Scripture.

One night as she was working at prying herself free from these chains, she cried out, "Lord, do open-heart surgery on me. Why do I always want to feel special?" In spite of this longing she found herself constantly brushing off people's compliments. It just didn't make sense. Suddenly the Lord made it all so clear: She realized what she really longed for—her dad to hold her in his lap, tell her she looked pretty, and cherish her. She cried and cried, mourning the absence of this kind of emotional connection with her father.

"Lord, bind me up. Put Your medicine on me," she cried out. Suddenly she felt God's love in her heart for the first time, although she'd been telling other people about that love for years. All at once, her self-hatred left and she no longer believed she wasn't worthy of being loved. Soon after this, she realized that Gary's temptation to look at pornography was not really her problem at all, but his, and she stopped blaming herself.

Their no-sex rule lasted only six months, but still Georgia didn't trust him. "Woo me," she suggested, "and make me fall in love with you all over again."

Meanwhile, God was setting the stage to deal with a key factor in Gary's part of the problem—his overwhelming passion for his hobby. Ever since he was a little boy he'd loved airplanes. He always looked up into the sky when he heard a plane, and his boyhood heroes were the crop-dusters who flew over his house on the farm. He'd spent long hours flying control-line model airplanes out in the pasture. But he'd put his hobby on hold to go to college, serve in the military, and get married. Then he again threw himself into his passion. Now he went to bed thinking about planes; he woke up thinking about planes. For fifteen years he had been completely and totally absorbed with them.

Gary designed and built one-horsepower model airplanes himself. He had his engines customized in Los Angeles, the wings fabricated in New Jersey, the fuel tanks in Kentucky, while he bought the fourteen-inch propellers from someone in Florida and the handles and controls from someone in New Jersey. He had the fuel blended and shipped to him from South Carolina in four-gallon lots. He'd spend four months building a plane, three months painting it and putting a glass-smooth surface on its five-foot wing span, and about a month trimming it out. *I'm not as fanatical as the really dedicated flyers,* he told himself to justify it all. The cost was immaterial. He worked hard—didn't he?

Gary flew his model airplanes in competitions, being judged on his plane's performance in a series of sixteen required maneuvers. He was a nationally ranked competitor in Control Line Precision Aerobatics and wrote articles published in airplane magazines. People called him from around the country to ask questions about the sport.

Although Gary was looked up to as a spiritual leader in the Barbers' Bible studies and prayer meetings, airplanes really owned his heart. Now after he and Georgia had been working on their marriage for a year and a half, a small aircraft came on the market at a price too good to pass up. He had always wanted to buy a full-sized plane. He and Georgia discussed it and agreed that they couldn't afford it. But he was planning to buy it anyway, so he borrowed five thousand dollars and soon the plane was his.

Although he had no peace that he'd done the right thing, he had a lot of fun flying it. But one windy day only two weeks later, he lost control and his plane crashed. Unhurt, Gary sat there in silence amid the whirling dust and wreckage. *I don't have to do this anymore,* he thought. The power that airplanes had in his life had sustained a mortal blow with the crashed aircraft, and he sensed he was on the brink of being free.

The healing process wasn't instantaneous. Georgia stood back and watched as her husband went through emotional withdrawal from his lifelong compulsion. She didn't want to get in the way, for God was obviously doing something in his life. It was so painful, it had to be from God. To Gary's astonishment, over the next week he actually felt relieved. This reversal amazed him, as he had always felt a compelling desire to do things with airplanes.

Soon after that, Gary and Georgia joined another church. There the Barbers found a level of worship different from any that they'd ever seen before. It was real. These people weren't just going through the motions. Gary felt he had been starving to death spiritually but hadn't even realized it. He'd been following the Lord out of a sense of obligation.

Although Gary's walk with God hadn't been exciting, he'd thought, *This is just the way it is. You just do it.* Having been a Marine, he believed you do what you have to do, no matter how you feel about it. But when he and Georgia began associating with believers whose lives pulsated with love for God, Gary thought, *I want this. I don't want a cold, regimented kind of Christian life anymore.*

A few weeks later while driving down the road, Gary became aware of a song in his heart. He was praising God. Three weeks had passed since any lustful feelings had taken over and driven him to look at pornography. *Something's different,* he thought. *But maybe this is just an aberration. I'd better wait and see.*

What he didn't realize until later was that addictions usually come in twos or threes. A person rarely has only one; for example, someone may progress from drugs to alcohol. In Gary's case, the crash ended his addiction to airplanes, and that healing then impacted his addiction to pornography. The inner force that had compelled him to sneak a peek at lewd pictures never came back.

Naturally, he's had temptations and he has stumbled in a few small ways. But he has not been consumed by a desire to look at pornographic pictures as he was before.[3]

During this time the Lord also broke through the Barbers' marital impasse. The trust between them began to return. Gary could give Georgia more of his heart because his aircraft no longer owned it. With Gary's affections no longer wrapped around his airplanes, the Lord could have the core of his being . . . and Gary could think beyond himself. He was released from something that had held him captive and he realized in a new way that there were people in the world besides himself. As his relationship with the Lord became more free, he grew increasingly aware that he needed to make his dear wife the most important thing in his life.

Weeks later, Gary realized, *I'm in a completely different place.* He'd be driving down the road and suddenly his heart would lift off in praise to God. This amazing surge came from deep within and was not calculated. A well-

---

[3] Unknown to Gary, his addiction to pornography had been a major reason Georgia sensed she did not have his heart, no matter what he did for her. "Men involved in pornography cannot love their wives above a three percent level," says John Regier, a marital counselor who has researched the issue.

spring of worship would just swell up inside him sponta-
neously. For the first time he understood John 7:38—

Whoever believes in me,
as the Scripture has said,
streams of living water
will flow from within him.

The plane crash, the healing of the Barbers' marriage,
and their dynamic new church all converged to produce
one great crescendo in Gary's life. He realized, *I'm living
on an absolutely different level than I've ever lived on before.*
And if he had to pinpoint one particular catalyst, he'd say
it was the plane crash.

"What I really loved was airplanes," says Gary. "My
heart was cold, and the things of God were blocked from
coming in, because my heart was held captive. When the
idolatry of airplanes broke, it freed up access to my heart. I
loved airplanes more than my wife. I was immature and
selfish. Most of my marital life was based on obligation
and what was in it for me. I would take Georgia out to
dinner. Rather than enjoy her, I was just fulfilling my obligation. Then I went back to what I really wanted to do—
play with my toys."

. The change in Gary affected every part of his life. He
had never realized how good a marriage could be or how
much joy a person could have. "In fact, much of the time
I hear a choir singing in the back of my head," he says,
"and I'm in constant communication with the Lord. I'm
very conscious of His presence with me all the time and I
often hear Him speaking to me." Now, during his sales
calls and whenever he faces a decision, he silently prays,

Jesus, what am I supposed to do here? Usually he senses the answer, or an event occurs that gives him clear direction.

The restoration of the Barbers' relationship took nearly two years, and the end result amazed Georgia. "Now there's much more freedom in our marriage," she says. "We have more of a oneness. We really talk and there's more depth. I have a deep trust and respect for Gary, and I'm not nearly as critical and complaining. I've come to rely on his God-given wisdom. In fact, my husband is a great guy. During intimate moments we talk and laugh and tease each other. It's fun. I love him for himself, not just because I need him."

As Gary breathed the fresh air of his new life, he couldn't stop thinking about the many men who struggle with the same issues—marital problems, pornography, and a hobby they love so much that it steals them from their families. So he volunteered to lead a seminar about pornography at a men's conference at his church. To his surprise, there was standing room only. Gary shared his own story in the allotted time, and after he finished, hands shot up all over the room. He finally had to stop answering questions so that they wouldn't miss lunch.

This first seminar culminated in Gary leading an annual program at his church to help men break free of pornography. Initially Gary hears men in this program say the same thing over and over: "If my needs are going to be met, I have to meet them myself." These men tell themselves, *Pornography is OK because my wife is not sexy in bed.* Gary points out how selfish such thinking is, showing them that it is a way of evading the necessity of dealing with the issues in their marriages. To think like that allows them to retreat into a fantasy world to get what they want.

"No one argues with you when you look at pornography," says Gary. "No one says no. This is self-centered escapism, because it bypasses having to deal with the difficulties of a relationship with a real person."

But as the weeks go by,[4] the participants change their tune. At that point Gary frequently hears them say, "I've never been able to talk to anybody the way I can talk to these men about this issue. And I've never had victory like I have now."

* * *

When Gary was trapped in a marriage to an angry, complaining wife, totally unable to break free of pornography's poisonous grip, obsessed with airplanes, living the Christian life by rote, he had no idea that his prison would force him to discover God as the great Deliverer. And having tasted that reality firsthand, he now finds that men flock to him for counsel. In the end, Gary's inner torment became his platform for a new life of partnering with God in the healing of marriages and ruined lives.

But if that were not great enough, Gary's personal life makes visitors to the Barbers' home long for more. His wife adores him. There's fun in the air at their house. And his children have been impacted by hearing repeatedly how

---

[4] Thirty men usually attend Gary's course, which lasts twenty-two weeks. Usually, after three months, men say, "Wow, I am in a bigger mess than just having a bad habit." Often they are battling anger and issues with their fathers. "We peel off the scab, and they see it is a far deeper wound than they thought," says Gary.

Each participant has to make a commitment to come to every single meeting, do all the homework, and contact another man in the group twice a week. They use the book *Pure Desire* by Ted Roberts, which includes a workbook and his own story of breaking free from pornography. To find out about conferences and resources, go to the website www.puredesire.org or call 1-800-234-0072 to order the book from East Hills Church bookstore in Gresham, Oregon.

God healed their parents' relationship. Someday when they face their own marital conflicts, they'll have the wonderful knowledge that God can break through any impasse they encounter because He did it for their parents.

Now Gary's walk with God has reached a peak that most Christians think is reserved only for saints they read about in church history classes. Relating to the Lord about everything, sensing His presence, knowing the guiding hand of the Omniscient One in decisions small and big, singing his heart out in sheer delight to his Creator, all are just normal fare for Gary.

Thus, the pain that propelled him into the arms of God became his ticket to a joy that just keeps getting better.

Part II

Fear

Chapter Seven

VILLAGE THUNDERBOLT

S ahn couldn't stand the pain any longer. She had to tell her mother how much her hip hurt. It had never hurt like that in all her seventeen years and she was badly frightened. If she couldn't help her family tend their mountainside opium fields, how would the family live?

As the months passed, a large, burning, swollen red lump developed on Sahn's thigh. All the neighbors in the village had their own ideas as to what caused it. "She must have been a bad person in her previous life," some said. "The gods are angry with her," others suggested. "If she does good works, she can stop it from becoming worse," a few volunteered.

Meanwhile, the priest at the village monastery weighed in with his opinion: "Your hands reveal that you have not honored your parents enough. You need to offer betel nuts

and tobacco at your family's shrine." Therefore, with great
effort Sahn stood up and offered rice and water with out-
stretched hands to the idols hanging from the shrine in her
house. But the red lump kept right on burning.

Sahn's parents were desperate enough to try anything.
They took their child to Mr. and Mrs. Schneider,[1] the missionary couple who came regularly to their village in Southeast Asia to translate the Bible into the local language.
"Please give us a pill to cure Sahn's leg," they pleaded.

"A pill won't cure this," the missionaries said. "You
need to take your daughter to the hospital down the mountain." This advice terrified Sahn's parents because people die
in hospitals.

But when Mr. Wisdom, a highly respected monk from
Buttertree Village, said, "You must have committed some
enormous sin or else you would have been better long ago,"
Sahn took drastic action. She set out to beseech the most
powerful gods to heal her. For people said that these stone
deities could suddenly weep real tears when a pilgrim knelt
before them, seeking help. So she took off on an arduous
route in the blazing sun, by ox cart, truck and dugout
canoe on a pilgrmage with fifteen others. After dragging
her leg up the endless steps to the huge pagoda, she knelt a
long time, face to the ground, pouring out her heart to an
immense Buddha. But he just looked down on her with a
stony smile and made no reply. Disillusioned, she made
her painful way home.

A few months later Sahn's mother finally gave up on
the neighbors' suggestions and sent her daughter to the
hospital down the mountain. The Christian doctor oper-

---

[1] Not their real names.

ated on her in vain. But as he prayed for her, he recalled a
drug which he had hidden away for emergencies, and with
this medication her hip and its festering sore healed. But
Sahn had sat on her little mat at home for a year by this
time and could no longer straighten her afflicted leg. The
doctor recommended that she go to the hospital in the
capital for help.

The next time Mr. and Mrs. Schneider arrived in the
village, Sahn's parents begged, "Will you please take Sahn
home with you and take her to the hospital?"

So the Schneiders took Sahn down the mountain and
along the rough road to the capital city. But the doctor there
couldn't restore her leg either. He could only straighten it
permanently and then she wouldn't be able to bend her
knee again. Everyone agreed that it would be better just to
let her hobble along on her bent leg as she'd been doing
for months.

Six months would pass before Mr. Schneider's work
schedule would allow him to take Sahn back home. Then
he and his wife would make the long day's journey on the
rough country roads to visit her tribe.

Meanwhile the Schneiders could hear Sahn screaming
in her sleep every night from nightmares. Demons
continued to harass her as her family at home had made
many pacts with evil spirits in an effort to get her well.
During the day the girl spent all her time daydreaming. In
vain Mrs. Schneider tried to teach her how to sew, embroi-
der, or knit, but Sahn wasn't interested. Meanwhile she
sorely tested the entire household by always wanting to
do something other than what the rest of the family was
doing. One by one, the members of the household began
to ignore her. The very fact that their cook didn't quit her

job demonstrated how godly she was.

Finally after three months Mrs. Schneider had reached the end of her rope and blurted out, "OK, Sahn, do whatever you want. I don't care anymore." The last person in the house who had been trying to reach Sahn had given up.

Later that evening, Mrs. Schneider went into the living room to retrieve a book. As she began to leave the room, Sahn called after her, "What can make my heart cool?" Her tribe expressed their need for peace in this way.

"You know," snapped Mrs. Schneider. "No one can do that but Christ."

"If Christ can make my heart cool, I want it," Sahn declared firmly. Surprised, Mrs. Schneider sat down as Sahn continued: "The more you would talk to me about sin, the more I laughed. I wanted to make you think everything was fine. But in my heart I'm burning and if Christ can make my heart cool, I'm interested. But I have a problem: Before I came here, the village elders warned me that I could go through the motions of being a Christian but I must not enter into Jesus. 'If you do that,' they told me, 'you will die.'"

Some time before, Mr. Schneider had led to Christ a woman in Sahn's tribe who was suffering from tuberculosis. The hospital had given her medication that proved lethal and she died. The village elders told Sahn that if the women had lived she would have been killed because she had entered into Jesus.

"So what should I do?" Sahn asked, her troubled eyes fastened on Mrs. Schneider's face.

"You have a choice," she replied. "You can enjoy peace with your neighbors now and live in hell for eternity or you can risk upsetting them for the time being and enjoy heaven with God forever. They may beat you—they may even kill you. The choice is yours."

"In my heart I'm already burning in hell," Sahn said firmly. "I want Christ." Then she described what had happened when she had poured out her heart to the smiling stone Buddha on her pilgrimage. "All a statue can do is smile," explained Mrs. Schneider. "It has no life. But God has life and He can judge us—but He can also forgive us, because He has compassion on us and loves us more than anyone else can."

As the two women bowed their heads to pray, Mrs. Schneider thought, *I'm making a martyr.*

As soon as Sahn had confessed how sinful she was and had asked Jesus into her heart, she prayed that her people could also come to know Him. That night she slept peacefully at last.

Mrs. Schneider and Sahn.

Sahn now became a different person. She helped clean vegetables in the kitchen. She discussed Scripture passages with the Schneiders and prayed with them. She listened with keen interest to Bible story tapes.

Sahn's tribe had never heard of specializing in one skill. Everyone planted and ate what he himself grew and each wove his own clothes. But Sahn now learned to knit sweaters and sold them, and with her profits she ungrudgingly paid for her food, at Mrs. Schneider's urging.

Mrs. Schneider also tried to teach Sahn to read, but the girl seemed to have a mental block against it. Then the missionary recalled a picture of a mother and child that Sahn had drawn. "Both of them have a black heart," Sahn had explained. That gave Mrs. Schneider an idea: *Sketches can communicate spiritual truth to Sahn even though she can't read words.* So whenever Mr. or Mrs. Schneider would tell Sahn about a passage of Scripture, they would illustrate it with a simple drawing in a pocket-sized notebook. Every morning and every evening Sahn would look at the drawings in her little book and have her devotions.

Galatians 2:20 became her favorite verse:

I am crucified with Christ: nevertheless I live;
yet not I, but Christ liveth in me:
and the life that I now live in the flesh
I live by faith in the Son of God
who loved me and gave himself for me.
(King James Version)

Mrs. Schneider drew a picture of the old Sahn in a tribal coffin to depict "I am crucified with Christ." Then she drew a red cross coming out of the chest of the risen Sahn to

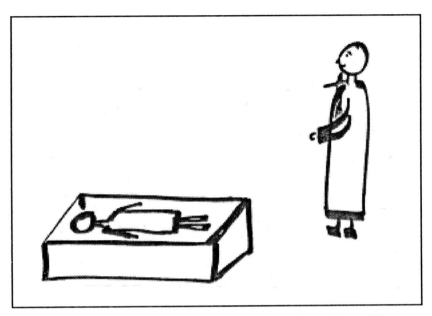

This is the actual picture Mrs. Schneider drew for Sahn to illustrate Galations 2:20. The line coming out of Sahn's neck plus the line pointing towards her chin are the cross coming out of her chest.

illustrate "nevertheless I live."

Despite the dramatic change in Sahn, she still lied. She'd lie for no apparent reason, for the people of her tribe viewed deceit as clever. After two months of battling this trait in the young girl, Mrs. Schneider asked her in desperation, "Why do you do this? There's no need to be afraid. Do you realize that every time you sin on purpose, you nail Christ to the cross again?"

Sahn knew that the Lord had died to make her heart cool. It crushed her to hear that her lies renewed the pain that He'd endured on the cross for her. She cried all night about it, and Mrs. Schneider let her. The next morning she prayed with a repentant Sahn, and the girl never lied again.

After enjoying life as a Christian for three months, Sahn

returned to her home village with the Schneiders. Excited, she hobbled on crutches up the narrow paths over rough, steep terrain for the two miles to the hut where her family lived while harvesting their opium crop.

The first night at home Sahn didn't dare pray. In her mind a person couldn't pray silently, for her tribe had no concept of privacy and she had always prayed aloud. She feared her stepfather's reaction, for she knew the tribal pattern: Usually stepfathers didn't tolerate the children from their wife's previous marriage.

But Sahn's peace of heart—the driving motivation for her conversion—had departed. The next day she thought, *If my stepfather kills me, so what? I can't stand this any longer.* So she thanked God aloud for the rice they were eating.

Her parents were alarmed. "Did you become a Christian?" they demanded. Sahn described what had happened. "OK, we'll pray to Jesus together," they decided. They usually offered food to the demons at the family shrine. Now they went outdoors and offered their rice to Jesus.

When Mrs. Schneider heard what had happened, she was concerned that they were using methods of demon worship to worship the Lord. "God says, 'What can you offer Me? The whole world is Mine,'" she explained to Sahn's parents. "What God really wants us to offer Him is our lives and hearts, not food."

Word of Sahn's conversion spread rapidly throughout the tribe. On the night the family returned to the village from the opium fields, the village elders cross-examined the girl and she clearly answered all their questions about her trust in Christ. Soon everywhere she went, people asked her about her faith, but her parents became frightened and stopped praying to Jesus.

Sahn's village chief with his family.

In that village, a week consisted of five days and every new moon marked the beginning of a new month. But Sahn kept a record of the days and went to the well every seven days to have time alone with the Lord. She talked about Him to the women coming to fetch water from the well, and prayed with them. They admired her courage and wanted to be like her.

· When the village held a festival to honor their spirits, Sahn left to visit her relatives who were interested in hearing about her new God. Back at the village, the spirits[2] communicated that if someone left the tribal religion, it would bring negative repercussions on the whole tribe.

---

[2] This is not a psychological state of mind; these spirits are real. They cause people to do destructive things. They inhabit people and speak through them with strange voices. In regions of the world where the name of Jesus has never been heard, activity of evil spirits is still common just as it was in the days of Jesus. See Mark 5:1-20 and Matthew 17:14-18.

Therefore, it was decided that Sahn must die.

As soon as she came home, the elders of her village received a message from Mr. Wisdom to relay to her: She must recant or lose her life. To silence her, they offered her a respectable position as a Buddhist nun. She refused. Right away the villagers became too afraid to speak to her so Sahn lived in lonely isolation.

A venerated elder who was Sahn's relative asked her to bring a food offering to the shrine and pray to the spirits. "I'm sorry," she told him respectfully, "but I cannot do that anymore." Her answer openly broke tribal law, proving to everyone how right it was to kill her. As soon as Mr. and Mrs. Schneider returned to the village, Sahn's mother begged them, "Please take Sahn home with you!" But the girl refused to go. "I know God wants me here," she insisted.

So before they left, the Schneiders drew a crown in Sahn's book to illustrate Revelation 2:10:

Be faithful even to the point of death,
and I will give you the crown of life.

The illustration of a crown that the Schneiders drew for Sahn.

The missionaries knew that Sahn might die, but they really didn't think the villagers would kill her as there was no precedent for such action.

A week later, Sahn served dinner to guests in her family's long, grass-covered hut, which housed ten families, on the edge of the mountain. As is customary for women, she ate late and then swept and cleaned the house before she retired. As she prepared for bed, she began to have a severe stomach ache. As usual, she opened her little book of drawings to meditate on God's truths before falling asleep—and woke up in heaven, for someone had poisoned her food.

During the six short weeks she lived for the Lord in her village, fifteen to twenty thousand tribespeople had heard of her trust in Jesus Christ.

Three months later, Mr. and Mrs. Schneider returned to visit the tribe once more. Women flocked around Mrs. Schneider, bombarding her with questions behind closed doors. "We know Jesus is real," they said, "because Sahn had a cool heart right up to the end and did not fear death. We want this too—but who will care for our children if the elders kill us for becoming Christians?"

Mr. Wisdom, who had led the decision to kill Sahn, now cast his lethal eye on a nearby village that was about to convert to Christ. "Are you not afraid?" he asked Timothy, the leading Christian influence in that village. Timothy had learned to walk with the Lord from Mr. and Mrs. Schneider, but recognizing a death threat when he heard it, he abruptly left the village and the ministry.

Mr. and Mrs. Schneider were devastated. Sahn had been martyred and Timothy had quit serving the Lord. In a few short weeks, Mr. Wisdom had wiped out the only Christian outreach to this unreached tribe.[3]

For three months the Schneiders did nothing but pray, fasting often, for this tribe. People around them began coming to the Lord, three or four per day.

Months later, some Christians visiting Mr. Wisdom's village observed the oppressive spiritual darkness there. "It's too much that one man can stand in the way of half a million people coming to Christ," they said. So they began to pray, *Lord, either remove this man or change him.* By the next day he was dead, although apparently he had been in good health. With his influence gone, people began putting their trust in Christ. The other tribespeople would ostracize these new Christians, but they didn't kill them.

* * *

When a young person dies, grief is more intense because people assume that this life which held such potential was cruelly cut off. But what is the purpose of long life? Is it not to make a positive, and hopefully powerful, contribution to the world? And that is exactly what God accomplished in six short months through the life of a seventeen-year-old.

In village after village in a mountainous region of Southeast Asia thousands of people heard of a person whose life demonstrated that a God named Jesus can make your heart cool. They were told that this young person considered knowing this Jesus more precious than life itself because she lived fearlessly in the face of death threats. Furthermore, her God was more powerful than all their spirits, for

---

[3] An unreached people group is a group of people who have no Christians living among them to show them the light of Jesus, who can pierce their darkness.

He took the life of Mr. Wisdom, who had led the charge against Sahn and anyone interested in entering into Jesus.

Thus, the Light in one person broke through the darkness in an oppressive corner of the world, revealing what happens when the forces of darkness and light collide:

> *The light shines in the darkness,*
> *and the darkness has not overcome it.*
> John 1:5 RSV

One little match in a pitch-black room cannot help but push back the darkness and enable people to see objects previously hidden. Sahn's light pushed back the dark evil fog in that mountainous region; for the first time the tribal people saw that the spirits they worshipped were not God and were powerless to give them what they craved—peace of heart.

Now, thirty years later, Sahn's influence lives on. For a radius of three hundred miles from her village, everyone knows of her courageous death out of love for Jesus. Today, pockets of believers exist up and down the mountainside because of an unchanging spiritual dynamic at work:

> *Unless a kernel of wheat falls to the ground and dies,*
> *it remains only a single seed.*
> *But if it dies, it produces many seeds.*
> John 12:24

Sahn's short life—because she was willing to lose it—is still producing many life-giving seeds.

Chapter Eight

THE LONGEST DAY OF HER LIFE

At nine p.m. that Saturday night Helen Crawford stumbled through her front door, exhausted. The day lay in a blur of unreality behind her—that morning she had run over her husband John with a truck. In confusion she relived the day over and over again in her mind. How on earth had this all happened?

It had started as such an ordinary day. The day before, the two of them had left Oklahoma City for a three-hour drive to the mountains to join their two grown children and their families who were spending the weekend in a ranch house there. Saturday morning John and Helen ventured into the predawn blackness. It was the first day of deer season, and their pickup was taking them to an area where they'd seen seven deer the day before. The prospects of getting a deer were good, and avid hunter that he was, John was excited by the chance. But their progress was slowed by the succession of gates, most of them having only wire for hinges, blocking the rutted lane. These were difficult to open and even more difficult to close.

When they arrived at the second gate, John shifted the truck into park as usual and stepped out to open the gate. Helen scooted over into the driver's seat as she had done a hundred times before, ready to drive the pickup through the gate and across the cattle guards while John closed the gate behind her.

But this time as John opened the gate, he heard the motor behind him rev up. *No problem*, he thought, unaware that the truck had begun to move toward him. It knocked him forward onto the gate, and John and the gate fell onto the cattle-guard rails as the truck's left wheel passed over him. It was the most intense pain he'd ever experienced and he was convinced he would die.

Forty feet beyond John's body, the truck came to a stop and Helen leapt out crying, "Oh, Dad, I'm so sorry! I'm so sorry!" They were mystified at what had happened. John had shifted the gears into park and Helen hadn't had time to touch them. The pickup just began to move by itself as soon as she slipped behind the wheel. Through the windshield she'd watched with horror as John fell forward while the truck passed over him.

"I'm alive! I'm alive!" he told her. "Pull me to the side of the road and go get Eric." Their physician son-in-law Eric was back at the ranch house, fast asleep.

"Dad, I'm not leaving you!" Helen insisted, thinking of the bears, coyotes and wildcats that roamed the area. "We have to get you into the truck." The left wheel of the pickup had run over the left side of his body, but neither wheel had hit his head. The bone in his left arm had been severed in two and his shoulder above the break had been crushed. Only skin and muscle were holding that arm to his body. In addition, his right wrist, right ankle, and three ribs were broken.

John's body lay blocking the gateway through which Helen needed to drive before she could take him back to the ranch house. She pushed and pulled his body over to the side but he still lay on the collapsed gate that had fallen under him. As she drove the pickup back over the cattle guard, the gate shook. "The pain was horrendous," he says.

She lowered the tailgate in order to pull John's body into the back of the vehicle. Yet, despite her proven athletic ability, she was not strong enough to lift him. His left arm useless, John used his right arm to pull himself up into the back of the truck, unaware that his right wrist was also broken. Helen lifted and pushed his pelvis, and together they succeeded in getting him onto a thin foam pad on the truck bed. Helen then drove as quickly and carefully as she could back along the rocky, bumpy cow path to the ranch house they had left a short time before. The fifteen-minute trip was sheer torture to John's crushed body.

He lay in agony, still convinced that he might pass out, or die at any moment. Helen heard his screams for help, over and over: "God Almighty! God Almighty! God Almighty!"

At once the Lord spoke to his heart with crystal clarity:

> *Don't blame.*
> *Don't complain.*
> *Don't feel sorry for yourself.*
> *Trust Me.*

John protested, *O God, You usually give these kinds of experiences to young men. I'm an old man!* He was seventy-eight. The Lord's reply was prompt:

John, I know how old you are. I can count. I'm giving you this opportunity because I love you. One more time you'll have an opportunity to trust Me.

The truck bumped its way onward up the mountain. Helen stopped at the ranch foreman's house and pounded on the door. "Jimmy Ray! Jimmy Ray!" she shouted. "John's hurt!" There was no answer. She pounded on the next door. "Keith! Keith!" The foreman's assistant came out immediately and as Helen left, he was calling an ambulance.

The sky was still dark as she drove up the hill to the main lodge and pounded on another door. Eric, her son-in-law, came out, followed by her daughter Bonnie. Hearing the story, Eric climbed carefully into the bed of the pickup and lay down beside John.

"Eric," John gasped, "do you have anything I can take for this pain?"

"I'm sorry, no," Eric said.

Although normally a quiet man, Eric talked nonstop to John as they waited for the ambulance from the nearest town, an hour's drive away. Knowledgeable about traumatic cases, Eric was trying to keep his father-in-law from losing consciousness, for if he passed out, he wouldn't be able to give them needed information and certain organs of his body would shut down.

The Crawfords were so deep into the woods that the ambulance, which was only a pickup truck, had trouble finding them. The foreman's wife met the rescuers and led them to the spot where John lay waiting. As they loaded him into the primitive ambulance, John asked the attendant for something to alleviate his pain. Putting his face right up in front of John's, the man said, "We ain't medics." And for one more hour John endured his intense pain en route to the hospital.

From the front passenger seat, Helen could sense the agony John was in. *O Lord, I need a verse!* she pleaded. And from the countless verses she'd memorized over the years, this one instantly came to mind:

> *Thou, O Lord, art a God*
> *full of compassion, and gracious, longsuffering,*
> *and plenteous in mercy and truth.*
> Psalm 86:15 KJV

Her heart cried out, *O Lord God, You are full of compassion and plenteous in mercy. Be merciful to John. Please do what You need to do so that he doesn't die.* The character of God, summed up in this verse, became her mainstay over the months to come.

They reached the hospital now well into daylight. "Ma'am, is it possible to get me something for this pain?" John asked the woman doctor attending him.

"First we need to find out where you're injured," she told him.

"That shouldn't take too long. I'll help you!" John quipped.

Carefully the medical staff cut off his padded coveralls with scissors the size of lawn clippers. They x-rayed him; miraculously, his body had not been punctured, nor had he lost any blood. But a deep black-and-blue mark stretched from his neck to the middle of his back.

Suddenly a highway patrolman arrived at the emergency room, and looking at John's back, he asked, "Was there malicious intent?"

Stunned, Helen protested, "None whatsoever!"

The patrolman looked intently at Eric and then at Jay, John and Helen's son. The two men shook their heads in disbelief and said, "No way! No way!" *I can't believe this,* thought Helen.

"His vital signs are great," the doctor finally announced to the family. "You can take him to whatever hospital you want, or we can treat him here." John prayed silently, *Lord, if I can't complain, I ask You for Mercy Hospital.* This Catholic hospital in Oklahoma City was near their home and there they would have freedom to pray with people and talk about the Lord.

"Take him to Mercy," ordered Eric.

And so they took off by helicopter, sparing John three more hours on the road. Once aboard, John lifted his right arm and realized for the first time that his right wrist was broken. *How on earth was I able to pull myself up on the tailgate of that pickup?* he wondered. *Angels must have been helping me!*

At one p.m. the helicopter landed on the roof of Mercy Hospital in Oklahoma City. At last they were home—or almost. Two of his best friends were waiting on the landing pad and others were already in the emergency room there. Seeing the concern etched on their faces, John attempted to relieve the tension in the air with his customary humor: "You know that guy who said, 'I feel like I've been run over by a truck.' I'd like to talk to him. I think I could help him understand." Then he added, "I'm really glad it wasn't an eighteen-wheeler." The men, shocked at his condition and hurting for him, laughed too hard in an effort to please John. They just couldn't enjoy joking about the agony he was in.

John Crawford.

By this time, people all over the country and across the world had been alerted to the accident and had begun a concert of prayer. John, himself, was continually asking the Lord for strength to endure the pain. Fresh in his mind were God's words to his heart as he lay in the pickup: *I'm giving you this test because I love you.* Finally after six endless hours of intolerable pain, he was given a painkiller.

When Helen finally opened the door at home that evening, the phone was ringing. Her friend Danna Humphreys and her husband were both on the line and they said, "We want you to know that you're a wonderful wife." Thinking that she might be filled with guilt about the accident, they wanted to reassure her. But anxious concern for her husband—not guilt—had been her overriding emotion all day. However, her heart had calmed down significantly ever since the Lord reminded her of His character with Psalm 86:15 in the front seat of the ambulance as they bumped their way down the mountain. It seemed that a lifetime had passed since then. And the next day, the deluge of cards, e-mails, flowers and gifts began. One couple sent a book or card nearly every day.

As John and Helen relived the events of that nightmarish morning, they continued to be amazed at God's grace in preserving his life. If the gate had been attached to the fence with hinges instead of flimsy wire, it would not have given way and the pickup would have crushed John's body against the metal bars of the gate, killing him. Then, if his body had fallen just three inches to the left, the wheels of the pickup would have crushed his head. Three or four inches to the right, and the low-hanging transmission and universal would have ground his head into sausage.

When the highway patrolman had questioned Helen earlier about the sequence of events, she had said, "My foot must have slipped and touched the accelerator." That was the only explanation that made sense to her, so that's what she had told him. Yet she had no memory of touching the pedals at all. Besides, in that event, the gears would have to be shifted from park past reverse and neutral, into drive. And she knew she had not touched the gearshift.

Later, one of John's visitors told him that several similar episodes with pickups of this make and model had been reported, with the vehicles suddenly lurching out of control. At last, the events were beginning to make sense. Though the Crawfords had been extra careful to adhere to the rules of safety all their lives, this bizarre accident had happened to them.

During the first days as Helen drove home from the hospital, she would often stop by the side of the road and sob uncontrollably. *Lord,* she would cry, *You are a God full of compassion and plenteous in mercy. I trust You to bring John through.* That first week it became increasingly apparent that John would live. But would he be disabled for the rest of his life? Would he ever regain the use of his left arm?

"Let's pray that your left arm will heal by itself and we won't have to operate," Dr. Steves suggested, for an operation would provide an easy entry for arthritis later on. So the family prayed while Dr. Steves strapped John's arm against his chest and left it there for three weeks. They never did have to set it, and the crushed and broken bone grew back together and healed on its own.

They did put a cast on his broken right wrist and operated on his right ankle to screw the bones together. "I've never operated on a man this old who was in such good shape," said the orthopedist with surprise. Three days after the accident John could walk on his cast, carefully supported on both sides by the hospital staff.

However, he was unable to feed himself, lift himself out of bed, or go to the bathroom alone. He often would need assistance during the night when the reduced staff was busy with other patients. So friends of the Crawfords hired an attendant to care for him each night from seven p.m. until nine the next morning.

Usually he had a different sitter every night. He delighted in sharing his faith with these helpers. When his pain became severe he would ask them to pray with him, and these prayers often led to a discussion about the Lord. One assistant was curious about his personal life. One day she asked, "John, how are you and Helen getting along?"

"We're having the most glorious time," he said. "I have the sweetest wife in the world. Why do you ask?"

"John! After all, she did run over you with a truck!" she exclaimed. Before this, it had never occurred to John to blame Helen for the accident and this was the first time anyone had implied to him that he should be bitter toward her. He lost no time defending his wife: "There's not a drop of impure blood in Helen's body," he explained. "For forty-five years we've traveled all over the world. We've been through all kinds of things together. I know she would never hurt me."

But his reply didn't make sense to the skeptical assistant. John had only one answer for that: "Let's pray," he said, taking her hand. And this time his sitter prayed too.

Shortly thereafter, Helen came to the hospital and said, "John, I know you don't want to hear this, but I want to say how sorry I am."

"Honey, it was an accident. Everyone has accidents," he reassured her. "There are multi-billion-dollar companies for people who have accidents. I'm going to give you an assignment. Take twenty minutes. Get before the Lord and settle it with Him. And leave it right there."

But Helen wasn't blaming herself. She had never felt guilty, because John had shifted the gears of the truck into

park himself before he got out. The truck's movement had been a freak event. She'd just felt the need to express empathy for all he was going through. Others also thought that surely Helen must be blaming herself. Their daughter Bonnie said, "I'm sure glad for Mama's sake that this

Helen Crawford.

accident didn't kill Daddy."

Some people marveled that she'd been able to help get him into the truck by herself. But fourteen years earlier, Helen had read an article about weight-lifting, where the writer had explained that a person who regularly lifted weights would be far less likely to fall and break a hip or another bone later in life. Helen then began lifting ten- and fifteen-pound weights for about five minutes a day, year after year. Now all that lifting paid off. Three weeks after the accident, when John came home, she could lift him up onto his feet by putting her arm under his right armpit. Without her weight training, her care for him would have been much harder.

John couldn't even lift his Bible to read, yet scores of Scripture verses he'd memorized over his lifetime constantly came to mind to nourish his spirit. As people prayed for him, God's grace empowered him to refrain from blaming anyone, from complaining about his pain and discomfort, and from pitying himself. It actually didn't seem difficult to him to trust God with the outcome of such a cataclysmic event.

As Helen faced John's long road to recovery, God encouraged her through James 5:11:

We consider blessed those who have persevered.
You have heard of Job's perseverance
and have seen what the Lord finally brought about.
The Lord is full of compassion and mercy.

This verse reminded her of an event long before when their family had been living in New Zealand. After their daughter Bonnie had made friends with another little girl, Helen began to talk with the girl's mother about the Lord. The woman flared up: "Don't ever talk about God to me again!" she snapped. So Helen didn't.

One day they were walking out of a building together as the wind and rain were lashing everything. "This weather would test the patience of Job!" exclaimed the little girl's mother.

Imagine that! thought Helen. *Thousands of years after Job's death, this staunch unbeliever has his name on her lips. Someday when I see Job in heaven, I'm going to ask him, "Was it worth it?"* And Helen was sure Job would answer, "Yes, it was worth it." Now as John recovered, inch by inch, she reminded herself of the perseverance of Job and the outcome. That motivated her, as the days passed, to persist in trusting God and helping her husband.

John would face still one more test: One day as he lay on his back on a therapy table at the hospital, his therapist said, "Lift your left arm over your head and lay it on the table." John could not believe his ears. This was the arm in which the bone had been severed in two.

"You're kidding, aren't you?" he asked. Her reply was firm: "No." She meant business. John was sure he couldn't do it. Nevertheless, he obeyed her orders and pain shot through his arm. His therapy sessions were becoming more trying.

One day the therapist told him, "This is our last day." He was to continue doing the exercises by himself at home. John was alarmed. He thought he might hurt himself trying to do something he shouldn't. But the doctor assured him it was safe and the test of will began.

Every morning John forced himself to do his physical therapy exercises for thirty minutes. Praying constantly for the Lord to help him, he would lie on his back on his bed, holding a one-pound weight in each hand, and lift both arms, laying them down over his head. For the first couple of weeks it was excruciatingly painful, making him cry. Then it got to the point where it merely hurt. He really didn't need to exercise his right arm, too, but "my left arm wanted company," he joked.

He didn't *have* to do those exercises in his bedroom but everyone had done all they could for him and now it was up to him. *Am I going to exert the effort to put myself back together?* he asked himself. *It is within my power. I could not prevent the accident. I could not assist the doctors. But I can be faithful to do these exercises.*

In his mind, John had a goal as he forced himself through the exercises every day. Dove season would begin on the first of September and he wanted to be able to swing a twelve-gauge shotgun and shoot birds that day. And as the weeks passed, all those prayers and all that self-discipline were taking effect.

"It is a truism that discipline works," John says. Officers who learn discipline in the military, he has noticed, are at a great advantage when they become Christians. Their habit of discipline carries over into the Christian life, and they benefit immensely.

John, also, benefitted immensely. Two months after the accident he could feed himself, put on his shoes and take a shower unaided. He and Helen even attended a wedding. One month later John spoke at a men's conference, and no part of his anatomy even hurt during the entire event. After three more months he was easily able to raise his left arm over his head, almost as high as he could raise his right one, and his right wrist was totally restored, although it tired easily. One doctor expressed amazement at how faithfully John exercised and at the extent of his recovery.

On September first—nine months after the fateful truck ride—John and two friends went hunting. Standing by himself on a hill, he shot at the first bird that flew by—and hit it! His deafening shout of victory startled his friends, standing a hundred yards away.

Two years later, John's son-in-law Eric told him, "From my medical experience I know that it's a miracle that you're functioning as well as you are. Many people your age wouldn't be able to function at all after such an accident. We've seen God do a marvelous work."

Looking back, John feels that it's too easy for older folks to slow down and coast if they have no more tests, no more mountains to climb, no more hurdles to overcome. For people feel good about themselves when they accomplish something. He believes Proverbs 13:19 KJV accurately describes human nature:

The desire accomplished is sweet to the soul.

"No sailor," John says, "brags that he spent the duration of World War II sitting in San Francisco. But he sure will tell you about his time at Guadalcanal! It lifts a person's spirits to know that God is still doing something in his life, giving him the privilege of looking to Him."

As John thinks back to what God said to his heart as he lay in the bed of that pickup—*I love you and I am giving you this test to walk through with Me*—he sees that the Lord was giving him a special opportunity to learn to trust Him on a deeper level, instead of just coasting along through life in comfort, as many people prefer to do.

* * *

Now with hindsight the benefits from John's severe trial come into greater focus. His family witnessed a powerful display of God's sovereignty in one split second: If the truck had hit John's body three inches to one side or the other, he would have died. As Eric and other medical personnel marveled at John's recovery, Helen saw God prove Himself to be full of compassion and plenteous in mercy. This trial thus brought them face to face with God's breathtaking character.

It's easier to trust God for someone else's trial than your own. It's easier to trust God for financial needs than for a rebellious teenager. But to see your body ripped apart, totally incapacitated, pushing you to the brink of death, that is a massive test of a person's ability to trust God. And yet John made a choice in the back of that pickup while he was shouting "God Almighty!" over and over. He did not choose to become angry or bitter at God. But during those six hours of pain so intense that he could have lost consciousness, he flipped an internal switch that said: I AM GOING TO TRUST GOD WITH THIS. And one seventy-eight-year-old man's confidence in God went deeper than ever as the Lord proved Himself worthy of His child's trust on a totally unpredictable journey.

John and Helen have spent their entire lives coaching people in the practical aspects of walking with God. There are countless Christians around the globe who point to the Crawfords as mentors who have played a significant role in their growth. On John's seventieth birthday one hundred of them gave him a surprise party in Oklahoma

City. Their gift? An envelope with a piece of paper in it. It stated that the Crawfords' mortgage had been paid off. Such is the extent of the gratitude and love that hundreds— probably thousands—of people feel towards the Crawfords.

These people not only prayed but also watched closely as John and Helen endured this trial. When life is tough, it is far harder to manifest godly conduct, and yet they saw John lay hold of God's grace so he would not complain while enduring excruciating pain at first and then constant aches and discomfort. They witnessed his devotion to Helen and his refusal to blame her whatsoever. They heard about him walking into his bedroom day after day to do those greatly dreaded exercises.

An example carries far more weight than words, even words of Scripture. To actually SEE someone live consistently makes an observer think: *If he can do it, surely I can too.* How many men have treated their wives more respectfully when trials came their way, remembering what John did? How many people have refused to complain when life became hard? How many wives have persevered, not because of Job's example but because of Helen's, when a family member endured a long-term illness?

In heaven we will all find out the answers to these questions. And John will become even more grateful that God chose to put him through such an ordeal.

Chapter Nine

OUT FOR A MORNING STROLL

Five-year-old Nathan and his little brother were cross. Every morning their big brother Weston got to go to school and they had to stay home. No fair! So this morning they vowed to go to school too.

Their daddy was off somewhere, flying airplanes. He was always flying airplanes and the boys wished he'd stay home. They didn't understand his job, flying high-altitude observation/surveillance planes over Korea for the United States Army. Their mommy, Julie, stayed home with them in their pleasant house behind high cement walls, but she was busy and they wanted to go to school. Not some other time. NOW! They were bored, playing in the dirt by the gate in front of their house. Lots of kids went to that school and every day they all got to play together. Weston had told them all about it.

Twice a week Mrs. Kim, their Korean housekeeper, came to help their mother and on those days this woman would walk seven-year-old Weston to the private school for foreign children that was so enticing to the little boys. That day they watched as Weston and Mrs. Kim started off for school. "Come on," whispered Nathan. "We can go with them if we stay behind. They won't see us and we can go to school too!"

So off they went, trailing Weston and his guide. When Mrs. Kim left Weston at the school, she set off for the market to do Julie's shopping, completely unaware of the two little shadows who'd followed her.

Meanwhile, back home Julie Sythoff had gone out to check on her two little adventurers, supposed to be playing in the dirt by their front gate. When she couldn't find them, she assumed that they must be over at the neighbor's, eating yogurt, as sometimes happened. She called the neighbor, but the boys weren't there. She began to panic. Although their house was located among kind people in a remote area, their quiet dead end did lead out into a long dirt road the length of a city block.

Frantically, she searched up and down the dead end and beyond to the long dirt road, scanning the area while calling their names over and over. She cried out to God for help. *Lord, give me wisdom to know how to go about looking for them,* she prayed. There was no way to predict where the two wanderers had drifted. She called her husband at the base, but of course he was out flying. She walked to the home of an American neighbor who had lived in Korea for a long time, but the woman wasn't particularly helpful. *Shall I call the Korean police?* Julie wondered. *My Nathan is a pretty smart five-year-old; he must be the one who thought up this plan, whatever it is.*

After fifteen minutes of fruitless searching, Julie knew she needed to go home to sit quietly and try to figure out what to do next. Suddenly from a distance, she heard Nathan's voice: "Mommy! Mommy!" She flew out the door and raced down the road. In her haste, she nearly collided with the two boys as they turned from the main road into the dead end.

She grabbed them both in a tight hug. "Where on earth have you been?" she demanded. "Mommy has been looking everywhere for you!"

"We went to school with Weston," Nathan told her. *They could never have gone to Weston's school,* she thought. *It's far too complicated to walk there on their own.* To get to the school one had to cross two dangerous paved roads connected by a maze of alleyways. The streets seemed to be laid out with no rhyme or reason. Even an adult who was unfamiliar with the vicinity could become quite lost in that area. How could two little troopers find their way there?

"We followed Weston and Mrs. Kim," Nathan explained. Julie knew that the way the housekeeper took was even more complex than the way she herself walked when she took Weston to school.

"Then how did you find your way home?" she inquired.

Patiently, Nathan explained. "We walked around some smelly water," he began. *That's those open sewers by the school,* Julie thought. *Maybe they really did go all the way over there!* "We were lost," he continued. "Then these two church ladies came up to us and said, 'We'll take you home.'"

"Church ladies!" exclaimed Julie. "What do you mean, church ladies?" On Sundays the Sythoff family attended an American worship service in the basement of a Korean church. A few soldiers and a couple of other military families also joined them, but the group was not large. Nathan knew everyone who attended these small fellowship meetings. Now he told his mother that he'd never seen these particular "church ladies" before.

The Sythoff family had lived in Korea for only a few months. *Nathan's memory must be flashing back,* Julie thought, *to the many American women he'd seen at church in the United States. But who in Korea could have been there to guide two small ramblers home?* Now Nathan was describing them: "They wore dresses and had curly hair," he explained, pointing up the street as though he expected to see them. *What IS he talking about?* Julie wondered.

"How did they know where we lived?" she asked. Her boys were not able to tell anyone their own address; their street didn't even have a name. She and Eric had not taught them how to find their own way home on foot, for the family went nearly everywhere by car. And Nathan certainly didn't know how to get to their house along the highly complicated route the housekeeper would have taken when she took Weston to school that morning. There was no way that Nathan could have told these "church ladies" how to get home from the other side of town.

"I don't know," Nathan answered.

"Were they Korean women?" Julie asked.

"What's that?"

"Did they look like our housekeeper or did they look like my American friend?"

"Our housekeeper," he said, not understanding how to detect the difference between races.

"Did they speak English?"

"Yes," replied the five-year-old.

So Julie and the boys walked back to the main dirt road
and looked in both directions to see if they could find the
"church ladies." But they saw no one.

"Do you think they might have been angels?" Julie
asked her small son.

"Prob'ly," he said, looking up at her.

The Sythoff family lived in Korea for one more year,
and in their small rural community where everyone recognized each other, no one ever appeared who met Nathan's
description. Until that point, Julie had felt many misgiv-
ings and much anxiety about her family's safety in this
foreign country. Frequent rumors that North Korea was
planning to invade the South to attempt to unify the country under Communism flew about among the citizens. Only
two hours of travel time separated Julie and her family from
the demilitarized zone and their enemies to the north. Eric
was often gone on flying assignments, and at times he was
required to attend conferences in Japan or the United States
for days, while she and the boys were left alone.

Although Julie had heard stories about angels intervening for others, it had never occurred to her that such supernatural protection sheltered HER family in that far-off place.
But Nathan's angelic "church ladies" had profoundly convinced her that a caring God controlled and shielded their
lives. Peace filled her heart and a strong confidence in God's
presence surrounded her for the remainder of their tour of
duty in Korea, enabling her to trust God for protection on a
deeper level in the years ahead.

* * *

Every mother guards against the terrifying possibility
that her small children could suddenly be left unprotected

in a world full of unimaginable dangers. Frequent news of children who have suddenly disappeared has made many a mother extraordinarily vigilant when her children are anywhere other than in a totally safe place. And yet because one mother let down her guard in a safe place, God stepped in to teach her a lesson that became a conviction for her whole family.

Most Christians believe in angels—the angels who sang to the shepherds the day Jesus was born, angels who protect missionaries in danger—but for everyday people, to believe in actual angels on the scene seems too good to be true. And verses about angels might be memorized or taught to children, but not really believed.

Then one day God gave a live demonstration that what He said about angels was literal:

> *He who dwells in the shelter of the Most High*
> *will rest in the shadow of the Almighty.*
> *He will command his angels concerning you*
> *to guard you in all your ways.*
> Psalm 91:1,11

From that day forward, a worrisome mother, who often enjoyed private conversations in her heart with the Lord, thought totally differently about her career as the all-day guardian of her children. She had assistance, divine assistance. She would do her job as well as she could, but if she slipped up, there was no longer anything to panic about. For now she KNEW that God's angels were under orders to protect her and her little ones. It changed everything for her. She could now rest because God's army of angels obeyed their Commander-in-chief. Thousands of years earlier King David expressed this reality clearly:

Praise the Lord, you his angels,
you mighty ones who do his bidding,
who obey his word.
Psalm 103:20

All God has to do is give the command, and His angels—maybe disguised in curly hair and church dresses—wing their way to perform their noble task.

Furthermore, as the years passed, the story about the "church ladies" by the smelly water was told and re-told in the Sythoff home. A decade after the incident, Weston, now a tall teenager, fell down some stairs. "Why weren't you hurt?" a family friend asked.

The Sythoff family (with their adopted daughter standing by Julie) in 1995, nine years after the angel incident.

"I don't know. Maybe some angels were protecting me." That concept just lived in his mind as a part of the real world as he knew it.

So one terrifying hour in Korea became the classroom to teach a mother and her family a great truth about God's faithful protection that once seemed too extreme to take seriously.

Chapter Ten

THE FORTUNATE ACCIDENT

That rainy afternoon, Sadi Nainggolan and a friend were deep in a game of chess, their eyes riveted on the chessboard. Close by in Sadi's attic bedroom, another friend was playing with Sadi's chemistry set. Being ignorant of the laws of chemistry, the boy was mixing chemicals, unaware that it could be dangerous if he did not follow Sadi's cautionary instructions. Suddenly as they began to react, he exclaimed with excitement, "Oh, Sadi! Look!" The friend tilted the flask in Sadi's direction and just as he rose from the chess game to see what was going on, the gurgling chemicals exploded directly into his face.

The shattering glass cut his friend's hand, but far worse, bits of glass flew into Sadi's eyes. He fell to the floor in shock and pain; everything became dark. No longer could he see the Indonesian countryside outside his window and he cried out to God.

Into Your hands I commit my spirit, Sadi prayed, using the very words Jesus prayed just before His death on the cross, for this high-school boy was sure he was dying. He prayed that the members of his family would come to know Christ. He prayed for many others he knew, assuming that he would soon leave this world and not see them again. After a few moments of blackness, Sadi realized that he was not dead but had been blinded by the explosion from his chemistry set.

He'd asked Jesus Christ into his life the year before, yet within a few months he'd lost interest in studying the Bible. But that night as he lay in darkness in the hospital, one verse he'd learned came to mind:

*Cast all your anxiety on him
because he cares for you.*
1 Peter 5:7

These words enabled Sadi (pronounced SAH-dee) to believe that God WOULD help him, even now.

The next day he recalled the story of Jesus raising Lazarus from the dead after his body had been in the grave for four days (John 11:1-44). *If Jesus could do that, He can help me more than the doctor can,* Sadi thought. And he placed his hope in Jesus with a determined act of his will.

The hospital staff prepared Sadi for surgery. He was worried. *What if the surgeon's hand slips during the operation? If that happens, I'll be blind forever.* In his helplessness he prayed, *Lord, all my life belongs to You. You can do anything You want with my organs. So I ask You to restore my sight.* This teenager believed that Jesus could actually do that, no matter how bleak the outcome appeared to be.

The surgeon proceeded to take eleven pieces of glass out of Sadi's left eye. It was so badly damaged that the surgical team removed it and replaced it with a glass eye. Later, Sadi overheard the doctor say, "There is a very slim chance that he'll ever see again with his other eye."

Nevertheless, Sadi clung to hope because of 1 Peter 5:7 and the story of Lazarus. He surprised the doctors by telling them that the power of God would restore his eye no matter what they thought.

During his three months in the hospital, he asked Badu Situmorang, the leader of the Bible study that Sadi had formerly attended, to come to the hospital. He knew he needed Badu more than he needed his own family, because his relatives couldn't comfort him on a spiritual level as Badu could. Sadi also asked his mother and younger brother to come and read the Bible to him.

He left the hospital, facing life as a blind man with few resources to go on with his life. But one day, Badu brought him a tape recorder that a young missionary had bought specifically for Sadi. Badu and his friend had recorded a cassette of the sixty verses of a Scripture memory course they liked. Hungrily, Sadi memorized every verse.

The two friends also recorded a ten-booklet Bible study for Sadi. He would listen to each recorded question, then the voice on the tape would quote the Scripture where the answer to that question could be found. The tapes enabled Sadi to complete the Bible study that he'd once considered not worth his time. Now it was food and drink to his very soul.

The following year, Sadi asked a blind person to teach him Braille, and then someone gave him a Gospel of Mark in Braille—a two-inch-thick stack of large, heavy pages. It became invaluable to him, and he read the book over and over to quench his thirst for God.

One day the Lord spoke powerfully to his heart through Mark 8:36—

> *What good is it for a man*
> *to gain the whole world,*
> *yet forfeit his soul?*

Suddenly Sadi wondered, *What good would it be if I did regain my sight but not live for the Lord?* He sat stunned by the very idea.

Previously he had aspired to become a mechanical engineer and make lots of money, but such a job entails laboratory work with engines and spare parts and would require good eyesight. Yet Sadi still hoped his right eye would recover so he could pursue his dream career. However, he didn't bargain with God by praying, *Lord, if You restore my sight I'll serve You.* Instead, he dared to surrender all his life and ambitions unreservedly to God, trusting Him to use him whether He healed Sadi or not.

The following year, the surgeon again operated on Sadi's right eye to try to clean out the remaining debris and minimize the damage. But the operation was not successful and the doctor told Sadi, "It's not reasonable to hope that you'll ever see again." However, he believed in miracles, and one of his relatives had a friend who was an eye doctor. So Sadi traveled to Jakarta[1] to consult him. This doctor performed yet a third operation, but afterwards, Sadi still could not see a thing.

Every day he pleaded with God to restore his sight. Sadi

---

[1] The capital of Indonesia.

participated in a Bible study and attended Christian fellowship meetings. At each of these gatherings he asked the believers to pray that the Lord would heal his right eye. His confidence rested firmly on the God who raised Lazarus from the dead.

Sadi then asked yet another doctor to operate, but he refused. Later, his resolve weakened a bit and he told Sadi, "I have to think about it."

"But I live far from here," the young man protested. "Please give me a hospital room while you mull it over." Sadi's persistent faith would not allow him to let go of even one possibility. The next day, the doctor decided to proceed.

After this fourth operation, Sadi could see shapes but not clearly. A lot of dirt still remained in his eye. "There is a special medication used to clean blood out of eyes after surgery," the doctor told him. "It's available in Singapore." Hearing this, the leader of the Christian activities that Sadi participated in arranged for a missionary traveling from Singapore to Indonesia to bring the medicine with him.

When the doctor applied it to Sadi's eye, at first people appeared like shadows to him. Slowly the shadows became more distinct. When he at last could even see faces, he was filled with indescribable joy.

But his mind was still tormented with a question: *How can God use me if I can see so little?* One day he prayed for an hour: *Lord, I have no other ambition than to be used of You. If You do not want to use me, then take my life, as I already have eternal life.*

Since God did not take that drastic step, Sadi kept looking for indications that the Lord was going to do the impossible, after all. And a month later, Sadi could read the headlines of the newspaper if he held it about four inches from his eyes. Now confident that his eyesight would keep improving, he registered to finish high school. He now wore glasses with lenses nearly half an inch thick and wrote his class notes in large letters. However, he was hampered because even while sitting in the front row in class, he could not make out what was written on the blackboard.

His progress continued and within a few months he could read a book held fourteen inches from his eyes, although he still could not read the blackboard. His vision remained cloudy as though someone had thrown dust into his eyes.

Now that he no longer lived in total blindness, he began to notice the huge work God was doing in his life through the experience: He had developed a close walk with God and eagerly told other blind students about the Lord. Four of them invited Christ into their hearts, motivating Sadi to punch out Bible verses in Braille to help them grow in their faith.

When he told his neighbors about the wonders of knowing the Lord, they listened to him skeptically. "If God loves you," they replied, "then why are you blind?"

That stumped him. *Lord, show me what to say so I can convince them of Your love,* he prayed. Although these neighbors felt sorry for him, Sadi didn't feel sorry for himself. He knew God truly loved him, and then he realized that his neighbors could not know the truth about God if they didn't want to do what the Lord wanted. For Jesus said,

If anyone chooses to do God's will,
he will find out whether my teaching comes from God.
John 7:17

Therefore, as long as those neighbors didn't want to obey God, Sadi knew it would be impossible for them to understand that God loved him whether his vision ever returned or not. He could not give them an answer that would satisfy them if they didn't want to trust the Lord. In fact, he now realized that he was not the only one whom others should feel sorry for. Instead, he should feel sorry for his neighbors who could not see the reality of God's love.

Furthermore, they couldn't grasp the threat of something much worse than not being able to see—the truth that had completely changed Sadi's perspective on his blindness:

What shall it profit a man,
if he shall gain the whole world,
and lose his own soul?
Mark 8:36 KJV

If they obtained everything in life that they wanted, but never found the Lord, the end of their lives would be tragic.

"When we're going through something difficult, our main concern is to get out of that situation," Sadi told a friend. "People make the mistake of thinking that if God helps them escape their trial, it's proof that He loves them. But that's the wrong mindset. Look at what Jesus prayed as He faced His coming ordeal on the cross:

Now my heart is troubled,
and what shall I say,
"Father, save me from this hour"?
No, it was for this very reason I came to this hour.
Father, glorify your name!
John 17:27-28

"Instead of just seeking a way out of our trouble, we should consider how we can bring glory to God in the midst of it."

Years later, Sadi tried to help a troubled college student entrust his life into the hands of Jesus. The student possessed both normal eyesight and good health, but he committed suicide sometime later. Merely being healthy wasn't good enough for him; he could not believe that God loved him and could make something good out of his difficult circumstances, even to the point of bringing glory to God.

After Sadi's graduation from high school, he entered the Institute of Technology in Bandung, choosing this school because the Christian organization that had helped him had a flourishing ministry in that city. He declared his major in math because it would be easier on his good eye than engineering.

His eyesight kept improving slowly. Now if his professors wrote in big letters on the blackboard and if there were good light in the room, Sadi could read what was written there. However, if the light proved insufficient for him to read the blackboard, he would swing into action and arrange for his classes to meet in another room with better light . . . except on occasion when a professor found it too inconvenient.

When Sadi's long journey to graduation was complete, he moved to a blue-collar town in East Java[2] to initiate a spiritual outreach to people in that area. He could have landed a more lucrative position if he had chosen to live in a prosperous city, but his values had changed: "I don't think I could be happy in any other job than one where I can share the good news about Christ and help new Christians grow in their walk with God," he said. And it espe-

_____

[2] Java is the large Indonesian island where Jakarta, the capital, is located.

cially excited him to go to this city because, after learning the local language, he would be working with villagers who had never been exposed to Christianity. A few other believers also moved there with him to band together as a team for greater impact.

Sadi could now see well enough to ride a motorcycle from the town to the village. During the rainy season, he was forced to push his bike through the mud,

Sadi Nainggolan, the miracle man, on his motorcycle.

park it far from the village, and walk barefoot to his destination through the mud. If it were raining when it came time to go home, he would have to spend the night on the floor of a hut because he couldn't see well enough to ride his motorcycle back to town when it was dark and raining.

These villagers believed in God's greatness, but thought of Him as far away and inaccessible. They expected Him to take vengeance on people who broke His laws. So Sadi and his team members pierced through their misconceptions by emphasizing two of the villagers' beliefs which were biblical—God is merciful and God is powerful. Sadi would tell the people, "Because God is powerful, He can come to us and become a man. Because He is merciful, He died for us." As a result, in less than three years Sadi's team saw thirty villagers decide to follow Christ.

Over the next seven years Sadi's good eye kept improving. The prescriptions for his glasses were changed seven times, and each time the lenses became weaker. He reached the point where, in good light, he could read a book at a normal distance from his eyes. He could even read large letters without his glasses.

Now, over thirty years after that fateful afternoon in his room at his boyhood home, Sadi leads a challenging Christian ministry in Solo, Indonesia. Sadly, his vision has now deteriorated to the point where he can no longer ride his motorcycle nor recognize someone standing just a few yards away. He cannot even read his Bible, but can read the Scriptures on his computer screen because the dark background makes it easier to discern the letters.

When his eyesight first started diminishing, after all the encouraging improvements over the years, his heart grew heavy. *It would be better if God just took me Home to heaven right now*, he thought. He remembered his two and a half years of total blindness in high school, when people ministered to him far more than he could minister to others.

So in 1995 he went to Singapore to have his right eye examined. The doctor told him he could not operate; the risk was too great. Sadi then sent his medical records to a doctor in the United States but he, too, could do nothing.

Then the Lord reminded Sadi of how much He had helped him ever since the accident and how much He had revealed His love through that tragedy. So Sadi surrendered the whole problem to the Lord once more. He decided not to doubt God's love or His good plan for his life. He resolved to quit thinking so much about himself and to hold on to 2 Corinthians 5:15 as the purpose for his life:

He died for all, that those who live
should no longer live for themselves
but for him who died for them and was raised again.

Today Sadi says, "My surrender to God has calmed me. I'm not shaken, thinking about what might come my way. I pray for those who are lost instead of praying for my eye, because so many people live in true darkness.

"The Lord is faithful and will continue to help me. He is more important than my eyesight or my life. Whatever happens to my vision will not alter my surrender to God, because His love for me is too great to be compared with anything else."

* * *

When a person has a huge problem that no man can solve, he faces an opportunity to find out how great God is and how much He loves that one individual. People often lose that opportunity by choosing to be bitter or to blame or to slink off to lick their wounds in a lifetime of self-pity, causing friends and family to pull away. Sadi could have chosen to blame his friend who didn't mix the chemicals according to his precautions. Or he could have become bitter and angry at God for letting the accident take place. Or he could have trusted in the medical profession to restore his eyesight and when it didn't happen, withdraw and live out his life feeling sorry for himself.

But the Lord's grace came streaming down on Sadi, and he seized the opportunity to trust God from the very beginning. A new believer who had hardly trusted the Lord for anything up until that point now began aggressively believing God to give sight to the blind. Sadi's faith grew explosively simply because he wasn't willing to accept the alternative despite one discouraging surgery after another. For his Jesus had raised Lazarus from the dead, so, of course, He would restore Sadi's vision. Sadi's confidence qualified him to get what he wanted because Jesus said:

> *Whatever you ask for in prayer,*
> *believe that you have received it,*
> *and it will be yours.*
> Mark 11:24

Mysterious things happen as a result of such persevering faith. And that was Sadi's experience: It just so happened that a missionary traveling to Indonesia from Singapore could bring the needed medicine to clean blood out of Sadi's good eye.

In that way he came face to face with the greatness of God—greatness demonstrated in one eye of one man who trusted Him. It happened quietly, in increments. After a long struggle, he finally could see shapes, then faces, then words on a blackboard, and one day he could ride a motorcycle safely in traffic. Sadi's reaction? To ride it wildly through the streets? No. He rode it to a village to share the news of a God so incredibly great that He gives sight to the blind and peace to the troubled.

If the accident had not happened, with Sadi's intelligence and capabilities it's doubtful that he would have chosen to learn another language and humble himself to minister to villagers—people with no exposure to the Gospel—so they could know Christ. Obviously, the accident had totally altered Sadi's values and long-term choices.

As if the accident were not bad enough, the Lord then let Sadi's long-fought-for vision slowly slip away. Why would God do such a thing? It seems cruel. However, by now many people knew Sadi and could observe him go through this new trial. They watched him come to a profound conclusion: *God's love is greater than having sight. God can be trusted to take care of His child.* Therefore, Sadi decided to focus on helping others rather than constantly praying for his own vision. He chose to go deeper in his trust of God and higher in his love for people, leaving his longing for sight on the altar.

How can something so nightmarish as the chemistry explosion produce something so marvelous? Because the One who orchestrates all things is a master at bringing something wonderful from the rubble. That's why it's reassuring to know that He said:

> *I form the light and create darkness,*
> *I bring prosperity and create disaster;*
> *I, the Lord, do all these things.*
> Isaiah 45:7

With the Sovereign One there's no such thing as an accident. Sadi demonstrates that by holding tightly to the Lord through a disaster, choosing to trust and obey Him, a person can become a theatre where God shows off His glory.

That's why the chemistry experiment that went awry was truly a fortunate accident.

Chapter Eleven

ONE AFTERNOON IN THE PARK

The weather was lovely as the gentle sunshine warmed the spring-like afternoon. This was not a day to stay indoors, so journalist Carrie Sydnor went to the arboretum, a huge tropical park in Nairobi, to relax and compose a song for some children on her street whom she led in Bible study. On a wide expanse of grass, she carefully spread her blanket and sat down under a big tree to let the tranquility and beauty of her surroundings help her find the words and melody that would enchant the children. Occasionally, some little monkeys scampered in the distance across the lawn, but no one was in sight.

Suddenly a man appeared, walking toward her. Where had he come from? No one else had been in the area. Smiling, he came up, knelt on the edge of her blanket and greeted her. Her pulse quickened, for this conduct often preceded a robbery. Coldly she told him, "I came here to be alone."

Undeterred, the man continued to try to engage her in idle conversation. In a firmer tone of voice, she said, "I want you to leave!" He smiled again, rose to his feet and sauntered off. But his insistent manner had frightened her, and for twenty minutes she was unable to focus her thoughts and continue her song-writing.

At last she finished the simple lyric and gathered her blanket, papers, Bible, and purse to take them back to her car. Realizing she still had half an hour before she needed to go home, she took only her car keys and headed back toward the arboretum to enjoy a pleasant walk in the sunshine. No one else was in sight.

For years she'd confidently believed that if she were to be attacked by an evil man, she would call out to the Lord to deliver her and He would. She knew well the promises in the Bible to prove it. While attending the University of Missouri School of Journalism, she sometimes discussed rape with her three girlfriends there. None of these women believed in Christ, and Carrie would confidently tell them of God's sure promises that she clung to for protection.

But then she heard stories about Christian women whom God did not protect in their hour of danger. She read about a woman missionary who had been gang-raped in Africa. This story shot terror to the very depths of Carrie's being. Later she heard about Lynn, who had been raped at gunpoint by her ex-husband. Lynn, too, had cried out to the Lord to save her but He hadn't. Such stories shattered Carrie's confidence and peace concerning the threat of rape. She no longer had answers and was tormented by recurring fear.

Now she was working in Kenya, as a journalist for a

Christian organization. As always, she read the Scriptures every morning, underlining phrases that spoke to her. As she had been reading the Psalms in recent weeks, the phrase "I will protect you" would often catch her attention. She'd underline it but she couldn't make herself believe the words. Suddenly one morning she cried out, "Lord! I'd believe You if only I knew what You meant!" Immediately He brought these thoughts to her mind:

> *Once a large group of people became so angry at Jesus that they wanted to throw Him off a cliff. But He walked confidently right through the crowd. No one touched Him. God protected Him for it was not God's will for Jesus to die that way. Also, such a death would not have brought glory to God.*

> *However, when the angry mob wanted to crucify Jesus, God did not protect Him because this death was God's will for the Father's great glory. For in that sacrifice, Jesus took all the punishment due me for my sins. I would not be able to go to heaven if Jesus had not died that horrendous death.*

Suddenly Carrie understood that in most cases, God does protect believers from evil people. However, on occasion, for His great and glorious purposes He lets wicked people harm one of His children, as when Joseph's brothers sold him into slavery when a caravan going to Egypt passed by. For God had a noble purpose in mind: Joseph rose to great power in that land and saved the Jews from starvation during Israel's famine.

As these thoughts flooded Carrie's mind, a feeling of

relief came over her. Now it all made sense. God could be trusted to protect her in times of danger. However, maybe someday she would be horribly hurt, but only if God had a great and glorious purpose in it.

Her long journey of fear finally came to an end.

Now at the arboretum in Nairobi, her new courage was about to be tested. As she strolled in the pleasant park, she saw a man walking toward her in the distance. As he drew nearer, she recognized him as the man who had walked up to her under the tree. He greeted her as they passed, but she remained silent and looked down.

Suddenly he grabbed her around the neck from behind and dragged her into the bushes. Instantly a verse she'd memorized long ago came to mind:

> *Call unto me in the day of trouble;*
> *I will deliver you.*
> Psalm 50:15

Carrie cried out in her heart for the Lord to protect her.

They landed in a clearing behind a wall of shrubbery. The man still held her firmly around her neck from behind as her legs stretched out before her on the ground.

"Why did you abuse me?" he demanded, using Kenyan street language which means "Why did you talk to me so roughly?"

"I thought you were a thief," she replied nervously. As if to prove his intent he demanded her money. But she had purposely left it in her car because of the prevalence of thieves in the city. He asked for her watch. She didn't own one. Then he demanded her running shoes; she kicked them off.

"I belong to Jesus," she told him, "and He will deal with you for this."

"I don't care," the man scoffed. Abruptly he rose and dragged her deeper into the woods. This time when they fell down, her back was on the ground and his hand was gripping her throat.

"I'm going to kill you. I'm going to kill you," he said over and over.

"I belong to Jesus," Carrie repeated firmly, "and He will deal with you for this." But her assailant didn't respond. His hand tightened around her neck and she could no longer breathe. She thought, *Oh, this is how I'm going to die. I'm not going to die of cancer or in a car accident.* Being under the control of an evil man had caused her to go into a state of shock, subduing her emotions and all her natural reactions. She closed her eyes and peacefully anticipated seeing the face of Jesus at any moment.

Suddenly he loosened his grip. "I've got your blood on my hand," he complained. *Well, what do you expect if you try to murder someone?* she thought. He was seated in front of her but to her surprise, he wasn't sitting on her legs. He began to talk of raping her. *Oh, I'm going to be raped,* she thought calmly, as if rape were an ordinary occurrence.

Matter-of-factly she told him, "I have money in my car. If we go there, I can give it to you." He seized the car keys in her hand. "You won't be able to find it in my car," she added. "I'll have to go with you to show you where it is."

He gave Carrie her keys back and stood up. "Don't leave or else I'll kill you," he ordered as he turned to go to the path where he had grabbed her. He needed to be sure there was no one there who would see them leaving.

"I won't leave," she assured him.

He took a few steps and turned around. "Don't leave or I'll kill you," he repeated.

"I won't leave."

He walked away. Carrie lay there, waiting for her attacker to return. *I think it's OK to sit up,* she thought. She looked around at the tall grass surrounding her. *You're in real danger,* she told herself. *You should be praying!* At once she cried out to God to save her.

After ten or fifteen minutes she realized the man wasn't coming back. *What changed his mind?* she wondered. She stood up and straightened her skirt. It was ripped and so were her stockings. Her index finger was bleeding. She had been pulled so far into the bush that she had to pray for guidance to be able to find her way back to the path again. As she walked past others on the way to her car, no one seemed to notice her ripped skirt or stocking feet.

I'm alive! I'm alive! Carrie kept marveling. Her impending death had been so real that she was shocked to be walking safely through the park. *What would have been left undone if I had died today?* she asked herself. Most of her projects now seemed insignificant except a book she was writing. She was doing it for a Christian leader to help believers learn how to share the Gospel with an ethnic group hostile to Christianity. In that moment she determined to make writing that book a high priority in her schedule.

When she reached her car, she was glad to put on her good shoes which she'd left there and numbly drove home. Right away she called her friend Susie O'Hair. "Susie, I was nearly raped and murdered at the arboretum an hour ago," Carrie told her.

"You're kidding," Susie responded.

"Susie, I'm NOT kidding."

"I'll be over at once."

As Carrie poured out the whole story, Susie said, "Carrie, you mustn't spend the night here alone. Come to my house tonight."

Late that night as the two women discussed the events that took place in the arboretum with Susie's husband John, he told Carrie that he'd heard a psychologist lecture on the way a woman should act if attacked by a rapist, based on research done on the behavior and mindset of such men.

To Carrie's amazement, she'd done everything the psychologist recommended without ever having heard any of it before. First, the psychologist had advised, "Be calm. Don't scream. That just spurs him on." Carrie had been amazingly calm. The psychologist had also suggested distracting the attacker, which she had done by talking about the money in her car.

It remained inexplicable why he hadn't returned to finish her off, and Carrie marveled at God's intervention. Surely He had protected her because of His faithfulness to those verses in Psalms that she had wrestled with.

On the evening the man attacked Carrie, she had planned to visit a Hindu family for the last time before they returned home to India. She had prayed that she would have a chance to clearly present the Gospel to them. When she called them to tell them the reason she would not be coming, they practically demanded that she come see them anyway, for they were so concerned for her. So before going to Susie's, she went to their house.

As she relayed to them the story, weaving in the details about trusting the Lord and what kind of relationship she had with Him, a room full of family members sat transfixed by her words.

After she finished, a four-year-old boy stood up in his chair and said frantically, "Auntie Carrie, you must always have police all around you wherever you go. Always, no matter where you go, Auntie Carrie, you must be sure that there are police all around you." Over and over he repeated his advice.

"Raja," she answered forcefully before the room full of Hindus, "you will never have policemen all around you wherever you go. But if you're ever in danger like I was today, cry out to Jesus and He will deliver you, too."

In the weeks that followed, Carrie reviewed time and time again in her mind the events that took place that one sunny day in the park. At the moment the man grabbed her neck, she didn't know if God would deliver her since she didn't know His purposes, but the Lord DID deliver her. It stunned her that God had somehow stepped in and moved her attacker to loosen his tightening grip on her neck and also convinced him not to return to the bushes where she obediently waited. *If God is going to protect me like that,* she thought, *what is there to be afraid of?*

Carrie Sydnor (Coffman) in Nairobi in 1983.

* * *

Although everyone knows he is going to die, it usually seems like a distant fact, especially when you're young and energetic. But after her encounter in the arboretum, Carrie's mortality seemed overwhelmingly real to her. She could lose her life just by a walk in the park! That gave her a whole new perspective. She had no guarantee how much time she had left so she had better use what she had now to the maximum advantage for God's kingdom.

In the following months Carrie worked hard on the book for the Christian leader, and today people all over the world are learning how to reach out in effective ways to the hostile ethnic group that he worked with. One highly respected missionary statesman told a meeting of missions-minded Christians, "If you're going to read one hundred books about how to share the Gospel with this difficult people group, Carrie's book should be the first one you read." The evil man in the arboretum could not extinguish the life of the author of such a strategic book for the spread of His kingdom.

Through a newsletter which Carrie sent out, hundreds of people heard the story of how the Lord had delivered her that day. They told others. Who knows how the story of God's faithfulness to protect His child impacted them in the years ahead when they encountered danger? And how did the story affect little impressionable Raja and his relatives in the future as they faced threats which their Hindu gods were powerless to protect them from?

Now as Carrie enjoys spending time with her grandchildren, she tells them stories about the great workings of God, including the story of how He delivered her that day in Nairobi. The first Scripture she helped them memorize was the verse God brought to her mind as the attacker's arm tightened around her neck and she felt him pulling her into the bushes—

Call upon me in the day of trouble;
I will deliver you.
Psalm 50:15

For she wants them to be prepared for some day of danger that is sure to loom in their future.

In this way God is continuing to use the terror of those few moments to teach many people that He can be trusted to protect them—the truth in Psalms that Carrie had had so much trouble believing years ago.

Chapter Twelve

UNEXPECTED BLESSING

The lights of the city spread out beneath the wings of the plane—Bangkok, Thailand! Their new home, so far from what seemed like home to them. The two children, four-year-old Richard and two-year-old Melanie, stirred restlessly in their seats. "Is that home, Mommy?" the four-year-old wanted to know. "Where's our house?"

"Hush, Honey, we'll find it pretty soon," Becky Mann reassured him. The children filled the air with questions:

"What is that?"

"See that funny house! Who lives there?"

"Why are they all riding bicycles?"

"Why do they wear those funny clothes?"

And again, "Where's our house?"

Answering their questions, Becky acted far more positive than she felt. When would they find a house suitable for them and finally get settled? And what would it be like to give birth five months later in a strange hospital in a strange land with a language still incomprehensible to her? How would she ask the doctor if the baby was all right?

Weeks passed as they settled into life in a new country with questions swirling in their heads. How do we cook this new food? Where do we shop and how? Gradually this strange new land began to feel more like home and soon the time came for Becky to deliver her baby. "You have a healthy baby boy!" the American doctor announced to her at the mission hospital.

However, the next day the pediatrician told Mike and Becky, "Your baby's blood test shows that he has an extra set of chromosomes. We had better do a second test to confirm the results." Those calmly spoken words shot fear into Becky's heart. *Surely it's a mistake,* she thought.

The next day while she nursed little Ryan, the doctors came into her room to tell her and Mike that their boy had Down syndrome. She looked down at her baby's beautiful face, trying to hold back tears. Mike reached out to hold her hand as they listened to the doctors. However, Becky heard nothing further that they said. *Why me, God?* she cried out bitterly in her heart. *Why us? Here we are in a strange land, serving You. Why this?*

Becky felt mired in hopelessness. God didn't seem near enough for her to hold on to Him for comfort. It didn't occur to her that God had given her Mike to hold her hand and share the sorrow and she was too absorbed with grief to remember her favorite verse, Philippians 4:6—

Do not be anxious about anything,
but in everything, by prayer and petition,

with thanksgiving,
present your requests to God.

The medical staff ordered more tests for Ryan and discovered that he had a good heart with no murmurs and that his lungs were developing normally. These were both good signs, as often Down syndrome children have serious congenital heart defects. But everyday Becky hoped that the doctors would come back to say, "The first diagnosis was wrong. Ryan is normal."

A week later Becky brought her baby home with a heavy heart. She called her mother, sisters, and brothers in California to tell them the news. But she didn't ask them to pray. She was angry at God. It wasn't fair that this new baby shouldn't be as healthy and normal as his siblings. Every night her agony continued. *Why me!? Why me!?*

She prayed but God didn't seem to be listening to her. She and her husband also talked to the Lord together and tried to comfort each other, yet their days were filled with silent despair.

Mike's mother had planned to come out to help care for the two older children for a time. When she got there, she realized the depth of her son and daughter-in-law's anguish and stayed longer than she had originally planned. A month later two of Becky's sisters flew into Bangkok to stay with the Manns for three weeks. The physical presence of these family members brought emotional support that Mike and Becky sorely needed.

Every time Becky held Ryan in her arms she felt the same deep love for him she had experienced with her other two babies. Contentment with this child filled her heart. His little smile lit up his tiny face and curved his eyes into crescent shapes. Anyone who saw him ended up smiling, too. His pleasant, patient disposition and calmness made him a special addition to their family.

When Ryan was two months old, Becky had to go back to language school from eight in the morning until noon everyday. But she found it difficult to concentrate on a new language, for she couldn't wait to get back to the house to make sure the housekeeper was taking good care of Ryan. Everyday she found him lying happily on his little mattress on the floor playing with his toys, or sleeping contentedly in his baby swing with its automatic rocking motion. Looking at him, she would think, *How could he have Down syndrome? He's perfect!*

Soon the pediatrician recommended that Becky and Mike take Ryan to a private hospital where they offered an early intervention program for handicapped children. So three times a week Becky and Ryan would take a thirty-minute taxi ride across town for his one-hour therapy sessions. These became Ryan and Mom's after-school activity and she appreciated the opportunity to practice her new language skills on taxi drivers, nurses, therapists and Thai mothers with their handicapped children. She began to see many unanticipated joys arising from these journeys.

Back in the United States Mike and Becky's family, friends and church members prayed for them. A steady stream of letters bringing love and encouragement kept coming from around the world.

One person sent them the video *Awakenings*. In this film, the mother said, "When we receive something good, do we stop and wonder what we have done to deserve such a good thing? But when something bad happens, we immediately demand to know why God has allowed such a tragedy." Suddenly Becky began viewing their situation in a new light.

The letters kept coming. Another friend wrote, "I will not cry *for* you, but I will cry *with* you. Someday God will replace those tears with smiles and laughter because God does love you, Mike, and your children. He loves Ryan so very much."

It soothed both Becky and Mike to read Psalm 10:14, quoted for them in another letter:

> *You, O God, do see trouble and grief;*
> *you consider it to take in hand.*

This flood of prayers and letters slowly made an impact on Mike and Becky's thinking. They put aside their reservations about God's plan for them and slowly came to understand afresh that God is gracious to His children just as Jeremiah had said:

> *"I know the plans I have for you,"*
> *declares the Lord,*
> *"plans to prosper you and not to harm you,*
> *plans to give you hope and a future."*
> Jeremiah 29:11

Becky's persistent question *Why me?* slowly came to be replaced with, *Why not me? Why not us?* The answer became clear to both Becky and her husband: When they surrendered to God's will and plan for their lives, He would give them strength and wisdom to face all the difficulties set before them. They began to rest on the reality of 2 Corinthians 12:9—

My grace is sufficient for you,
for my power is made perfect in weakness.

When they let God be God in choosing what kind of baby they had, they began to experience the incredible peace described in Philippians 4:7—

The peace of God,
which transcends all understanding,
will guard your hearts and your minds in Christ Jesus.

Slowly Becky realized, *I can either choose to be mad at God or I can choose to dwell on God's words and be satisfied with His promises.* She decided to adopt a totally different attitude and simply obey what God said to her—

Have I not commanded you?
Be strong and courageous.
Do not be terrified;
do not be discouraged,
for the Lord your God will be with you
wherever you go.
Joshua 1:9

Furthermore, the Lord assured Becky that He would not forsake them no matter what they faced with Ryan . . . and she chose to take His words literally:

I will never leave you nor forsake you.
Joshua 1:5

Of course, there would be extra expenses raising a handicapped child plus unexpected, trying emotional situations. How would they deal with the unknown demands looming in the future? Then God quieted Becky's heart and convinced her that He could be trusted to provide for whatever they needed as they raised this unique child. Believing an old familiar verse settled the issue for her:

My God will meet all your needs
according to his glorious riches in Christ Jesus.
Philippians 4:19

All of these circumstances comforted the Manns deeply—the scriptural passages that God led them to, the words of encouragement and verses in the letters they received, the presence of family members who had traveled great distances to be with them in person. Certain old

Mike and Becky Mann with their children in 1999 (Ryan, front, left).

familiar truths came into sharper focus and strengthened their spirits as well: "God has a plan for Ryan and for each member of our family," says Becky. "God is not only powerful, but loving and kind. Nothing can separate us from the love of God, not even a severe handicap. One thing I have learned through all this: I can always praise God in joy as well as in sorrow."

Today Ryan, age eleven, is doing well in the third grade. His parents view him as a special gift from God, as his gentle and simple ways have been a sweet blessing to each member of their family. "I am thankful for Ryan, just the way he is," says Becky. "I am thankful for God's goodness."

* * *

Fear probably shoots through every pregnant woman at the slightest indication that her baby might not be normal. To discover in the hospital that something drastic is wrong with your child is an extremely emotional pain added on top of the high physical price the mother has just paid to bring her baby into the world.

However, today any anxious expectant mother can watch Becky and witness unmistakable evidence of God's astounding grace. Not just her words but her countenance and attitude reveal that she *is* thankful for Ryan just the way he is, that she *does* believe that it was good of God to give her this handicapped child. The Lord can rebuff any mother accusing Him of not being loving because her child was not born normal; all He has to say is: *I bring before your court of judgment Exhibit A—Mike and Becky Mann.*

Becky will meet thousands of women in her lifetime, who will wonder silently if not openly how she handled it when the doctor told her that her boy had Down syndrome.

Even if these women don't hear the full story, they will see that God did something extraordinary just by watching the Mann family relate to one another.

Isn't that what people who love the Lord long for God to do through their lives? God chose little Ryan to be the agent of such glory for Himself and, in so doing, put Mike and Becky through temporary anguish.

The anguish gave them another gift: "Pain is God's megaphone," said C.S. Lewis and the Manns' pain made them unusually sensitive to the truth in familiar verses. They could not remain dejected and depressed, for as they believed these passages of Scripture, they infused new LIFE into Mike and Becky just as King David said it would:

> *I will never forget your precepts,*
> *for by them you have renewed my life.*
> Psalm 119:93

No matter what happens to Becky and Mike in the future, they have etched deep within their psyche the memory of God not just restoring them in their days of despair, but giving them delight simply through coming into contact with the life-giving power of the Word of God and taking it seriously.

In such a shaky world, who knows what the Manns will face in the future? They are well prepared to go through anything because they have experienced a wellspring of strength that can bring them out on top no matter how severe the blow.

Part III

Chapter Thirteen

THE QUIET THIEF

Rod Sargent was the talk of the whole headquarters at the Christian organization where he worked. Handsome, articulate, godly—he was everything a woman could desire except for one thing: He was a confirmed bachelor. Single women often eyed him with interest, sometimes sure that God had told them that this particular guy was the man for them. However, the years passed and he seemed unmoved by any of them.

Then a lovely twenty-four-year-old brunette named Diane came to work at the organization's Colorado office and suddenly this unmovable bachelor was no longer outside the reach of women, especially this one.

As time went on, their friendship deepened and they were married.

One day some years later, Diane was having lunch with

Rod and Diane Sargent on their wedding day in 1966.

her good friend Gladys Trumble. Their friendship ran deep, and their children enjoyed playing together. Sometime before, Gladys had battled breast cancer, and her doctors had performed a mastectomy. Now a year later the cancer had returned, this time to her liver and she had been told that her liver looked like Swiss cheese.

"How can you accept this so well?" Diane asked Gladys that day. "Aren't you worried about your children?" At the time they were five and seven.

"I know the Lord will take care of them," Gladys responded calmly. "It's God's will that I go through this experience." Previously Diane had watched someone close to her face the possibility of cancer with mind-numbing anxiety. Gladys was the first Christian Diane knew who was going through such a harrowing trial, yet was handling it with confidence in God's goodness and control of the situation.

She watched her friend endure the entire ordeal. Diane

would often drive Gladys to the hospital for her arduous chemotherapy treatments. "Talk to me! Talk to me," Gladys would beg, "so I don't think about what's coming."

Despite the most aggressive treatments available, three months later Gladys died. Diane marveled at the peace that filled her friend to the very end even though she was leaving her children behind. Troubled, Diane prayed, *Lord, are You preparing me for something?*

Before Gladys left this earth for higher ground, Diane's husband Rod began experiencing debilitating illness and pain. "I don't know what's wrong with you," his doctor said, "but it's nothing horrible. You'll just have to learn to live with it, whatever it is." Yet Rod kept getting worse, so he and Diane sought a second opinion. X-rays showed that he had a blockage in his small intestine, and the doctor decided to do some exploratory surgery.

He tried to be reassuring: "There are seventy thousand cases of colon cancer every year, but there are fewer than a hundred cases of cancer in the small intestine. So you probably don't have cancer."

Diane was not prone to worry. She would not rehearse possible negative scenarios in her mind ahead of time, but would wait until she knew the facts before she began fretting. Besides, she really did not think Rod had cancer.

During his surgery the next day, she sat with friends in the waiting room. Afterwards, the doctor came out to tell her that the blockage turned out to be cancer after all. The surgical team had removed twelve inches of Rod's small intestine. Diane felt like she had been hit by a truck. But her friends who were sitting there began praying and by the end of the day a wonderful peace from God had come over her. The frantic feeling had left.

The night after the surgery was one of the loneliest nights of her life, but she also felt it was one of the most significant. She was in Rod's hospital room at his bedside; all their friends had left. Rod had fallen asleep and, left alone with her thoughts, she could not believe she was going through this trauma alone. "Rod, wake up!" she longed to say.

Then the Lord spoke to her heart: *Diane, you have known and studied about My love and sovereignty for years. Now will you accept it as true for you and Rod and your children* [ages eight and eleven] *whether he lives or dies? Are you willing to accept that whatever happens is My best for each one of you?*

That night Diane made a decision that would determine the course of the next eight years of her life: She chose to believe that whatever happened, God was in control of it . . . and that as the situation played out, it would in fact become the best that God had for each member of her family. She rested her emotions and stability on that truth and slept peacefully the rest of the night there in Rod's room.

Again and again as the days passed she returned to the truth of God's sovereignty and good intentions for her family, which had so powerfully gripped her in the hospital room that night.

Diane's sister had been caring for the Sargents' children over the weekend of Rod's surgery. Their son and daughter then came to the hospital but were not allowed in their father's room. They had to wave to him from the doorway, their sober little faces emphasizing the grief that had touched their young lives.

Elise and her big brother Rodney knew that cancer kills people. Their playmates' mother, Gladys Trumble, had died of cancer just the week before. Rod and Diane couldn't

pretend that this was something to be taken lightly.
Back home, little Elise began
to cry. As Diane put her to
bed, she prayed, "Dear Lord,
if it's Your will to take my
daddy Home, please do it
softly without much pain."

Their family life was
never normal again. For a
year, Rod had chemotherapy
three times a week through
an IV in the back of his hand.
After a break of three weeks,
he would go through the

Rod Sargent, five years before
cancer struck.

ritual again. The powerful chemicals would bring him
severe nausea and debilitating weakness. The whole experience was so emotionally unsettling that he couldn't
drive by the hospital or look at the place where the needle
was inserted in his hand without feeling waves of nausea.

One of Diane's biggest concerns was how this experience would affect their children. Would they begin to hate
God? She knew that the way she and Rod reacted to events
would play a big role in how the little ones would respond.
She and Rod were real and the children saw their tears, but
they too had to learn to walk with God through this trial.

At last Rod completed his chemotherapy treatments. A
year later the doctor again did exploratory surgery and
found a little more cancer. The surgical team removed it
and told him they thought he was now cancer-free.

Amazingly, Rod and Diane never lived in dread during
this whole period. However, they had tasted how fragile

and hard life can be. Diane realized, *If Rod does die from cancer, I will be alone with the Lord. I have got to know Him so much better than I do now.* So she began studying the Bible in depth to find out why people suffer and how God uses such hard times in their lives. One day a week while her children were at school, she would pore over the Scriptures. In the past she had participated in numerous group Bible studies, but this was the first time she had studied the Scriptures because she needed it so badly. She now dug into the Word totally for herself, for her own desperate need.

Her hours of study had a profound impact on her. She came to know God in a way that she had never known Him before. Once she realized that she was growing to know Him deeply, a great hunger spurred her on to keep searching the Scriptures.

Before the study, Diane had thought of God as a super human being. Then as the Lord grew bigger in her perception, she found it so much easier to trust Him. She learned that God always uses suffering for our good if we let Him. For example:

Joseph suffered.
    It deepened his character.
        It developed his trust in God.
        God then used him mightily.

Moses suffered.
    It deepened his character.
        It developed his trust in God.
        God then used him mightily.

Paul suffered.

It deepened his character.
It developed his trust in God.
God then used him mightily.

Diane came to feel the same way that Job did at the end of
his ordeal:
*My ears had heard of you,
but now my eyes have seen you.*
Job 42:5

To her amazement, as the way she knew God expanded to
a level she had never experienced before, she came to agree
with the apostle Paul, who said:

*Whatever was to my profit I now consider loss . . .
I consider everything a loss compared to the
surpassing greatness of knowing Christ.*
Philippians 3:7-8

This truth brought her to a profound conclusion: Whatever is necessary for us to grow to know Christ has to be
for our good.

After studying the subject of suffering for a year, she
became so excited about the wonderful results that God
brings out of suffering that she actually wanted to suffer
more. She even desired that her life would become more
difficult so that she would be forced to trust the Lord to a
greater degree, to walk closer to Him and to depend more
on Him.

One day God gave her that opportunity. As the
Sargents' children reached junior high school, they went
through struggles that made Rod and Diane trust Him in

a new way. They learned to accept that God loved their children more than they did and that He could be trusted to be faithful to take care of their children's needs.

Five years after Rod had been declared cancer-free, the scourge returned. The doctor said, "The cancer is in your stomach and has attached itself to the abdominal wall. It's also in the lymph nodes in your groin." Obviously, no one can live without his abdominal wall and therefore, the surgeon could not cut out the new malignant tissue. If he did, he would also have had to remove Rod's leg, for the cancer had impacted the leg's circulatory system.

Lord, I just can't be strong enough for what's coming! Diane prayed. *So You'll have to be strong for me.* After that, every time some new complication would come up or a test result would be bad, she would turn around into the Lord's arms and draw new strength from Him.

In all of this, Diane was discovering the reality of Job 36:15 (emphasis hers):

> *Those who suffer*
> *he delivers **in** their suffering;*
> *he speaks to them **in** their affliction.*

This truth became her daily experience. Scripture had never been so alive to her; she was more sensitive to the voice of God than she had ever been in her life.

At that time Diane read a book called *Don't Waste Your Sorrows,* by Paul Billheimer. The author explained how people usually just grit their teeth as they go through a difficult situation until the trial is over. However, he says, they are missing their opportunity to grow in their relationship with God. A person has a choice—to resist the pain of the experience and its lessons or to trust God and learn.

The Apostle Paul also said that his hard times had come to him for that very purpose:

In our hearts we felt the sentence of death.
But this happened that we might not rely on ourselves
but on God, who raises the dead.
2 Corinthians 1:9

No one knows what he trusts in until his faith is tested, Diane discovered. She became convinced that growth consisted of turning to God more and more quickly when something bad happens. She even came to a place of being content with whatever came into their lives—another stay in the hospital, unexpected bleeding, or something else. She learned to accept that this was what God had given them for that day and she didn't have to understand it.

Contentment didn't come from floating along on a tranquil cloud of placid emotion. It came in the middle of pain and struggle, when they accepted each situation as God's best for them and asked Him to use it in their lives. Each day as the news about Rod's health became more and more troubling, Diane was actually able to be content.

When events of life go badly, people often ask, "Why me?" But Diane thought, *Why not me? Why should we be exempt from pain and suffering that most people, including Christians, go through? 'Man is born to trouble.'[1] That is just the way life is. Our bodies and our relationships have problems, and these are just part of living in a sinful world.*

People would often say to her, "We know that God is

---

[1] Job 5:7

going to heal Rod." He and Diane had discussed whether they should pray that, but they never felt that the Lord was leading them to do so. After one more person told Diane of his confidence that God would heal her husband, she thought, *How strange that they know that, while the Lord has never told us.* In frustration she prayed, *Lord, how should we be praying? Should we be asking You for healing?*

The Lord spoke to her heart, *No, just pray for My will to be done, and that I will be glorified in your lives.*

Again and again Rod was in and out of the hospital. Once when he had been there for quite awhile, he called his wife at home. "Come and get me," he said. "The doctor told me I can come home." He was in tears—and he was not one to cry. But the hospital was such a lonely place.

The week before their son Rodney left for college he said, "Mom, when Dad had cancer the first time, I thought, *I couldn't live if he died.* But now I know I can make it."

"What do you think the difference is?" she asked him.

His reply filled her heart with joy: "Now I know I can make it with the Lord."

A short time later, Diane was preparing to give a talk to some Christian women and as she gathered her thoughts she became overwhelmed by what God had done in her life through Rod's battle with cancer. "Sweetheart," she said, "you know I've benefitted greatly in my relationship with the Lord through these past seven years. But you're the one who has borne all the pain, sickness and suffering. Can you honestly say that all that has been worth it because of what God has done in our lives?"

He was silent for a moment as he sat thinking. Then very quietly he said, "Yes."

As their ordeal continued, Diane prayed one day, *Lord,*

what do I do now? God answered her in 1 Peter 4:19—

Those who suffer according to God's will
should commit themselves
to their faithful Creator
and continue to do good.

Through this verse the Lord told her, *What's happening here is for Me. You didn't cause this. Trust Me. Get your eyes off yourself and get your eyes on other people.*

In December Rod returned to the hospital again. On the seventeenth she asked his doctor, "Can Rod come home for Christmas?"

"He can come home anytime you want," he replied. *Oh, his case is hopeless,* she realized. *They can't do anything more for him.*

Rodney came home from college for Christmas vacation. Now the whole family knew Rod was dying. "You need to go to your dad," Diane told her son, "and tell him anything that you feel you must say to him—because you may not get another chance." That visit was the last time Rodney saw his father.

Periodically a nurse would come to take a sample of Rod's blood and send it to the laboratory. After one test, the results showed that Rod's kidneys were shutting down. Diane thought, *It won't be long now.* But a week later they did another blood test. "His kidneys are working again," the medical staff reported. Diane thought, *Oh no! How much longer?* Rod told his wife, "This is like looking down a long, dark tunnel—and there's no end to it."

"What's the purpose of all these blood tests?" Diane asked the doctor.

Surprised, he answered, "To let you know what's going on."

"If it doesn't matter," she said, "could we not have any more blood tests?" The emotional yo-yo was too much for all of them. The doctor complied with her request.

Soon the medical staff had a hospital bed sent to the Sargents' home to allow Diane to care for Rod there. She would set her alarm and get up every four hours to give him morphine through his IV. "I'm not a nurse," she said. "I don't like nursing sick people. But this was something I could do for him."

One day her sister, a nurse, stopped by for a visit. "This is the way it should be," she told Diane. "People should be able to die at home, surrounded by those they love."

Diane was surprised at her own calmness. "It amazed me that I didn't wake up with panic during this time. The Lord helped me sleep without being terrified."

Before Rod's illness, Diane had focused on the present. But now she began to look at life with an eternal perspective. God opened her eyes to a new reality:

Though outwardly we are wasting away,
yet inwardly we are being renewed day by day.
For our light and momentary troubles
are achieving for us an eternal glory
that far outweighs them all.
So we fix our eyes not on what is seen,
but on what is unseen.
For what is seen is temporary,
but what is unseen is eternal.
2 Corinthians 4:16-18

As Rod lay in his bed dying, she would look at him and say, *God, if what Rod is going through is light and momentary in comparison to the wonderful things You have prepared for him, I cannot begin to imagine what it's going to be like in heaven. O Lord, give me an eternal perspective!*

Soon Rod began to breathe in a certain cycle. He would take a deep breath, a smaller one, then a smaller one, and then an even smaller one. At that point he would begin the cycle all over again. This is not unusual for people about to die. The family was prepared for the end; they didn't want him to keep living this way. When the visiting nurse came that Friday she said, "I'm going away for the weekend and I don't think he'll be here when I come back."

Diane asked the Lord that when Rod died she could be there beside him. One Sunday as she combed his hair, he took a deep breath . . . a smaller one . . . then a still smaller one. Yet this time he didn't take another deep breath as usual. She stood there beside him, filled with a great peace and relief that the Lord had taken him Home. He was sixty-three years old; his children were sixteen and nineteen.

Rod's funeral was the last thing Diane could do for him. Just like his life, she wanted the service to glorify God.

People had been telling her, "You're so strong. I could never go through this the way you are." Such comments frustrated her, as she knew the praise was misplaced. Finally she was able to make it very clear in her short talk at the funeral: "Rod and I are not strong people. But we have learned what it is to be strong in the Lord."

* * *

Rod's end came. A totally different woman emerged from the fire of his death. Isaiah 48:10-11 explains why:

See, I have refined you, though not as silver;
I have tested you in the furnace of affliction.
For my own sake, for my own sake, I do this.

That was seventeen years ago. And the gold that God produced in Diane while in that furnace still shimmers. Although she is unusually beautiful, the soft glow on her face is what people notice. The Lord gave her a treasure in the fire that she always carries, for time does not diminish gold purified in intense heat.

God proved that He does, in fact, send trials for our good—and He demonstrated how He does it through the life of one little woman whom He made breathtakingly wealthy by walking with her through the shadow of death.

Note: Two years after Rod's death, the Lord led Diane to marry another godly man, Jerry Kindall of Tucson, Arizona.

Chapter Fourteen

THE ORPHAN

Suddenly, nineteen-year-old Esther Waruiru couldn't be
certain of anything. Her father's recent death had
shaken her to the core, bringing into question all she
believed. *What kind of a God would take my father who lived to
serve Him?* she wondered. *How could a loving God do such a
thing? Does God even exist?*

She'd never met a more loving person than her father.
Men just wanted to be around him. He'd bring crowds of
people to their home in the Kenyan countryside, and his
wife and daughters were continually making tea for the
stream of guests. Esther's mother also had a depth of character that attracted to her their nine children as well as many
women in their church. These two parents naturally taught
their offspring about the Lord, for He was so central to their
lives. Now Esther attended a Christian boarding school

where she continued to learn about Jesus Christ.

She had just returned from her Easter vacation and a precious time with her father, who wasn't well. During Kenya's cool months he sometimes did not wear warm enough clothing while riding his motorcycle, aggravating his asthma, and eventually this had landed him in the hospital. Then a short two weeks later her brother had appeared at her boarding school to tell her that their father had unexpectedly died. The words "I know that my Redeemer liveth" from Handel's *Messiah* had kept going through her head, preserving her sanity as she packed to go home for the funeral. *Because the Lord lives, my father lives,* she had told herself.[1]

Now back in school, alone in her anguish, Esther took long walks every evening around the compound of her boarding school and poured out her heart to God, even as she questioned if He were really there. *It doesn't matter that I've been following You all these years,* she told Him. *Dad served you all his life. How could You do this? Now I need You to make Yourself real to me and show me that You are who You claim to be in the Scriptures so I don't doubt You anymore. If You do that, it won't make sense* not *to follow You. Otherwise, Lord, I'll go my own way.*

With the motivation drained out of her, she quit studying her hardest subject—chemistry. She attended class and did all the practicals, but neglected the systematic study necessary for the final exams. By the end of the day she just didn't have the strength to care any more. But before long she realized that if she failed chemistry it would break

---

[1] See Appendix A to understand why Esther could be so sure this was true for her father, a committed Christian.

her mother's heart, and that alone motivated Esther to force herself to resume studying. She passed chemistry, but just barely.

None of Esther's friends could understand what she was going through. None of them had lost their father, and Esther felt totally alone in her anguish. For the next three months she continued her solitary evening walks around and around the compound. Soon she sensed Someone walking with her. They carried on conversations. "Lord, You are in heaven," she said out loud one particular night," and this down here is the arena of men, playing the game of life. You just move in on us occasionally. How do You expect us to know You?" His reply was as clear as though it had been spoken aloud: *That's why I gave you My Word.* After that Esther approached the Scriptures with a sense of awe and anticipation.

She emerged from this black period a different person with her faith now based on unshakable truth. God seemed utterly real to her. *If the God revealed in Scripture is really who He says He is,* she concluded, *then it does not make any sense NOT to follow Him.*

But as soon as Esther graduated from high school, her mother was hospitalized. She'd suffered from a weak heart for years, and now she had a heart attack. The doctors gave her only three months to live. So Esther returned home to nurse her mother, care for her two little sisters, and supervise the family coffee farm. She went on a partial fast for two months—eating half portions at meals, drinking a beverage in place of lunch—while praying constantly that God would restore her mother's health. For Esther's love for her mother ran so deep that she could not find the words to describe it.

You know, God, Esther said one day to the Lord, *If You take my mother, You can have anything else in my life. Nothing else will be worth holding on to if I lose her.*

But as the days passed, Mrs. Waruiru's face became swollen and she seemed to be nearing the end of her days. Esther stopped eating altogether, fasting and praying for God to spare her precious mother's life. For she remembered what Jesus had said to His disciples who were frustrated because they could not cast an evil spirit out of a tormented boy:

> *This kind can come out only by prayer and fasting.*
> Mark 9:29

Then surely she would see God raise her mother up in good health by prayer and fasting. Jesus said so.

However, two days later as she sat by her mother's bed in the hospital, Esther heard her mother sing a song she'd never heard before. The ethereal voice seemed like someone else's, and her mother seemed already en route to heaven. The next day she died with a smile on her face, relaxed and at peace. She was forty-seven years old.

Later that day Esther knelt beside the still form at the mortuary and prayed, *Lord, I know You can bring her back if You want to.* She looked intently at the body she'd loved, but the woman didn't wake up. After the funeral Esther's older sister Mary and her husband took the two little sisters to raise them, and their cousin came to run the coffee farm, freeing Esther to go to university.

But Esther didn't want to go to university. She now felt even more tormented than she had after her father's death. Keenly aware of God's presence, she did not doubt His existence this time. The months of leaning so hard on the Lord for her mother had drawn her unusually close to Him. Yet she severely questioned the reality of His love.

The pain of loving someone deeply and then losing her went just too deep. Esther could not imagine being able to cope if it ever happened to her again. Therefore, she decided not to allow herself to give herself to totally loving someone again, for God might soon take that person away, too. She stopped reaching out to members of her family and made no effort to keep her many friendships alive. She purposed to need no one, erecting a wall around herself. Carefully she controlled how much she cared for others and refused to extend herself beyond a certain point. *I'll figure out how to run my own life without pain*, she thought. *I don't need closeness to anybody.*

However, now that she knew in the core of her being that God was who He said He was in Scripture, why wouldn't a person want believe in Him? Therefore, she felt that the best thing she could do for her peers at university was tell them about Him so they could know Him, too.

Esther struggled for a year to accept the fact that her mother indeed had died. She suffered from splitting headaches, but doctors couldn't help her and urged her to see a psychiatrist. *God, I don't have any confidence in psychiatrists,* she prayed. *You heal me or I'll just have to endure the headaches.* The Lord heard the cry of His hurting child and healed her.

One day during a conversation with a theologian about her mother's death, Esther said, "I felt that God told me during my time of prayer and fasting that He would heal Mom. But He didn't. It's obvious that fasting and prayer don't work."

"But He did heal her," the man replied. "He gave her the ultimate healing." His words startled her and made her see that her mother was now living a far happier life in heaven. That comforted her to a degree. Nevertheless, for years it continued to be too painful for Esther even to think about her mother's death.

Although students at the university could make a request to room with a good friend from high school, Esther kept to her plan to avoid intimacy and remained aloof from her former schoolmates. But the university assigned her a roommate whose insecurity demanded Esther's involvement with her. The roommate had lost her mother at an early age, and uncaring aunts had raised her. Everything frightened her, even going to the dining room alone. She wanted to do her laundry only when Esther did hers, and couldn't even go to town by herself to buy soap.

Lord, I can't believe You did this to me, said Esther. God was using this needy roommate to force His child to step out of her self-built fortress. Esther did extend love to her and they developed a lasting friendship. The whole experience taught Esther that the world was full of needy people starving for love. Although she did gradually let down her guard to a degree, she remained cautious in her relationships.

One day on campus she met a Swedish missionary named Lena Hagegaard, who recognized Esther's neediness, and extended herself to this hurting student. Initially Esther tested Lena's love by not allowing her to come too close. Then one Friday Esther arrived at a women's weekend conference to find that no other students had shown up. So the two women spent the night there alone.

The next evening Lena listened as Esther dared to open

up and share her problem of doubting the love of God. As the two of them knelt together and prayed about it, somehow the Great Physician reached down and touched Esther's aching heart, and from that time on she no longer struggled to believe that God loved her.

But she did keep wondering, *Why did God take both my parents in one year?* She considered, for the first time, that in the light of her parents' close relationship to each other it was far less painful for her mother to be able to join her father quickly. But then she would remember how her mom wanted ten more years to raise her two last children.

The intensity of Esther's struggle over her mother's death became the tool God used to teach her about His nature. *God's love is not explained by our experiences,* she realized. *It's there and it's real. I did not bring my parents into this world, but God did and it is His prerogative to take them when He wants.* Then she remembered a profound thought that a wise Christian had once shared with her: "God is consistent, but He is not predictable."

In addition, the Lord seemed to be teaching Esther constantly about His love. One key Scripture He used was Jeremiah 31:3—

> *I have loved you with an everlasting love;*
> *I have drawn you with loving-kindness.*

Furthermore, she realized God had already proved His love by Jesus' death on the cross. As a result, whatever happened, her security began to be found more and more in that love that she had once decided did not exist.

After her graduation, Esther joined another young woman living with Lena and began teaching anatomy at a

veterinary technical school. The women took turns preparing dinner each evening, and when Esther didn't have
to cook, she loved to lie in bed and read a novel, content to
be alone. However, the bed of one of the women stood
parallel to Esther's. Suddenly she realized that God had
forced her into a corner where she had to relate to another
person. *I have no right to isolate myself,* she concluded one
day. *I have a choice. Am I going to open up and extend myself
in love to my roommates or not?*

She purposefully set out to teach herself to think of the
needs of others, and every day for a week she looked for
something to do for her roommate that day. She sought to
pattern her mind to think from the other person's point of
view and it did not take her long to learn to observe what
someone else needed.

She also learned that the way people related to her
affected her own disposition, giving her insight into how
she affected others. One day as she walked up the stairs, a
new thought struck her: *I don't have to behave according to
my moods. I can make a choice to behave lovingly regardless of
how I feel.* Deciding to change her conduct toward other
people infused her with a new sense of total freedom.

The purpose of Lena's mission organization[2] was to
teach students how to help their friends put their trust in
Christ and then instruct these new believers in how to live
out their faith. Esther knew how to lead others to Christ,
but she did not know how to help them walk with the Lord
on a daily basis. Drawn to Lena's love and the practical
ways she and her colleagues were teaching women to coach
new believers, Esther quickly became an eager member of

[2] The Navigators, whose international headquarters is located in Colorado
Springs, Colorado, USA.

Esther Waruiru in 1985.

the group.

As she applied her new discoveries she developed some deep convictions: "You can't win people to Christ and disciple them if you don't love them deeply. To influence people that profoundly totally depends on loving them. In an office job you don't have to let people into your life. But if I purpose to win them to Christ, it won't work unless I let them into my heart. People must be the focal point of a ministry that's developing disciples of Jesus Christ. It's God's decision how far they move into my heart."

* * *

Seeking answers at God's throne and from the Scriptures, as Esther did during her time of grief, became a pattern in her life. Today, several decades later, she is known all over Africa for her wisdom and depth in the Lord. Her opinion is sought out. When the Lord took both her parents, He was shaping a woman of God to influence a continent just as He put a teenage boy through a long ordeal when He was shaping a ruler for Egypt who would save the Jews from starvation.[3]

Long after Lena Hagegaard returned to Sweden, her mark could be felt in Kenya because of the women who followed in her footsteps. In Esther's case, instead of withdrawing from relationships, she has extended herself first to women students at the University of Nairobi, then later to working women, and in time to countless African believers who see in this person someone who can give them wise counsel.

Nearly twenty years after Esther's parents died, she was participating in a Bible study with a few of her peers. One intelligent woman expressed her concern that, when she related to people, she would not be bored. Esther, perhaps a more intelligent woman, quietly commented, "My concern when I relate to people is that I be loving."

Wisdom is rare. The ability to trust God is a great gift. But to love, that is the greatest. And love became the trademark of Esther Waruiru's life. Such is the beauty that God fashioned in the core of one Kenyan woman because He was not afraid to let her be burned by fire.

[3] See the story of Joseph in chapters 37-50 of Genesis.

Chapter Fifteen

WHITE-HOT FURNACE

What on earth has happened to me? Elizabeth Demkin wondered as she woke up early one snowy morning. Her head throbbed; her whole body felt as though it had been through a war, though rarely had she ever had a headache.

As the cobwebs of sleep fell away, she recalled what had happened the day before. She had stopped at a stop sign when her neighbor's heavy car had skidded helplessly on the ice and crashed into her smaller, lighter car. The two of them had stopped to review the damage. "Oh, that's not so bad," they reassured each other.

But now Elizabeth realized that something dreadful must have happened to her body. Attempting to get out of bed was so painful that she lay there without moving. During the night, three feet of snow had fallen in northern

Virginia, and the entire area was paralyzed.   Immobilized
at home, Elizabeth endured her pain for days until it was
possible to get to a doctor. His verdict—a whiplash. But it
was no ordinary whiplash; it had upset the delicate bal-
ance of the side-to-side curvature of her spine.

Gingerly, she left his office clad in a neck collar and
grasping a prescription for a painkiller and muscle relax-
ants. But the medications proved ineffective and, as the
weeks turned into months, her pain didn't subside; she was
forced to resign from her part-time job. Yet over time her
body eventually responded to chiropractic treatments until
she came to the point of having only an occasional headache and could go back to work.

One day two years later her two boys wanted to go
swimming. "Please, Mom," they begged. "It's so hot!"
Together they went to the pool to enjoy a family time. As
Elizabeth moved through the water, the flippers she was
wearing seemed to weigh her feet down, and she arched
her back to lift them closer to the surface. Suddenly,
intense pain shot through her back. *Oh, no!* she thought.
Now what have I done to myself? Grasping the side of the
pool and supporting her back with her hand, she climbed out.

This time chiropractic treatments, physical therapy and
medication all proved ineffective. Keeping her job as a
school nurse meant enduring daily pain in her lower back
and all the way down her right leg to her toes, and by the
time she came home in the afternoon, she could barely make
it to bed. From there, she'd give her sons instructions, while
her husband Joe ran the household and cared for the boys.
Meanwhile, Elizabeth would lie in a sea of pain, fighting to
keep her spirits up by listening to the Bible on tape hour
after hour.

Six back surgeries and twenty years later, Elizabeth's pain remained, but she had become a far different person. She had found an exquisite treasure: "God's Word has been so freeing," she says, "even though at times I have felt as if I were in prison in my own body. To study the Scriptures has been like eating food every day; it's life itself to me. It's as if I live on two different levels—experiencing physical pain, but God's Word is healing me IN that pain." Naturally she would not choose pain for herself, but she came to understand why King David said,

It was good for me to be afflicted
so that I might learn your decrees.
Psalm 119:71

"It's good that I'm afflicted," she says, smiling, "for it led me to God's Word."

Elizabeth found that as she put the right things into her mind, it affected her thoughts, her behavior and even how she felt. Her personal batttlefield was her mind, not her body. She would even force herself to go to church where she would lie on the floor in the back of the sanctuary so that she could participate in the service, for it gave her hope in the awesome character of God.

Each time Elizabeth went through the ordeal of yet another surgery she expected it to free her

Elizabeth in her body cast at the beach after her first surgery.

from pain. Many people laid hands on her, praying that
God would heal her. Yet the Lord never did. In fact, some
Christians judged her: "Why aren't you getting well?" As
happened countless times, God Himself led her personally
to an answer in Scripture: Even the great apostle Paul had
a severe ailment—a thorn in the flesh—which God did not
heal (2 Corinthians 12:7-9). *God doesn't heal always everyone,
at least not in the way expected,* she realized. *It has nothing to
do with a person's spiritual condition.*

In fact, she discovered that many great people of faith
suffered horribly even to the point of death (Hebrews 11:36-
39) for a high and lofty reason:

God had planned something better.
Hebrews 11:40

These verses enabled Elizabeth's heart to rest, for she was
learning that God had a noble goal in mind in choosing to
let her pain remain.

As the years passed and the hurdles increased, Elizabeth clung to the Lord so tightly that she acquired a sweet
intimacy with Him. She sensed the Lord was caring for
her and controlling her circumstances even though it looked
like they were out of control. When her surgeon could find
nothing in her x-rays to indicate why her pain continued,
he concluded that her problem must be psychological. He
sent her to a psychiatrist who prescribed an antidepressant,
but to her despair, one of its side effects was permanent
impairment of her memory.

Chagrined, she turned to the book of Job for comfort.
His pain was also very great. His friends also questioned
him, saying, "What's wrong with you?" His story made

her realize, *Nothing can happen to me unless God allows it, for He allowed Satan to do what he did to Job.* She knew that the Lord had her best interest at heart. It was His character to be good. So it put her at rest to discover that God—not her surgeon or psychiatrist—was orchestrating her circumstances:

The Lord gave,
and the Lord has taken away.
Job 1:21

"Nothing can happen to us apart from God's choice," she told a friend. "He can choose to do what He wants. Why do we complain when He gives and then takes something away? God is still wonderful, nevertheless." This realization became a rock under her feet.

When a subsequent operation revealed the physical cause of Elizabeth's unrelenting pain, her doctor-appointed psychiatrist was mortified and apologized to her. Then he gave her some advice that would affect her outlook for the rest of her life: "Don't develop a pain personality." For he had had numerous clients who could never get beyond focusing on their pain. His words made an indelible impression on her.

Whereas before she had viewed pain as her enemy, she came to see it as her friend. For through it she could identify with the suffering Jesus went through; she was experiencing what the apostle Paul experienced:

I want to know Christ and the power of his resurrection
and **the fellowship of sharing in his sufferings.**
Philippians 3:10 (emphasis hers)

She identified with how Jesus felt when He cried out to His Father in the Garden of Gethsemane to deliver Him from the coming crucifixion. For many times she had cried out to God to deliver her, too. That understanding and identity with Jesus in His suffering drew her into a sweet closeness with Him.

In addition, all her back surgeries forced her onto a path of trusting God on a deeper and deeper level, manifesting a courage that she did not naturally have. It all began before the first operation when the doctor told her about a patient of his who had undergone the same surgical procedure and had become paralyzed afterwards. Eventually he committed suicide. The story terrified Elizabeth and came back to haunt her before one operation after another. Each time God spoke to her afresh to trust Him in this one, too. And she would hold tightly to the verses He gave her, such as:

Have I not commanded you?
Be strong and courageous. Do not be terrified . . .
for the Lord your God will be with you
wherever you go.
Joshua 1:9

She took it literally that God would be with her and that gave her all the courage she needed.

Finally when she was going in for the fourth surgery, she prayed, *Lord, if paralysis is Your will, it's not the worst thing that could happen; my life would not be over.* At last she could trust God more than her fear; she could accept whatever He had for her, knowing that the surgeons were not in control, God was.

In the midst of Elizabeth's difficult circumstances, the

Lord would send her just the right advice, making a significant difference in her progress. For years she had been spending fourteen to sixteen hours a day in bed. Then a friend told her of the energy she'd received from drinking a product called Barley Green. Elizabeth started drinking it daily and miraculously, it got her out of bed.

At another time her pain level put so much stress on her body that her digestive system began to deteriorate; she could no longer digest food and began to lose weight. A woman at church recommended a Christian nutritionist who knew exactly what to do. Like a diabetic who must take insulin, Elizabeth began taking capsules of digestive enzymes after every meal and immediately she began gaining weight and her energy increased.

Then she noticed that God was playing out the truth of 1 Corinthians 10:13 in her life:

When you are tempted,
He will also provide a way out
so that you can stand up under it.

Several times when she'd been tempted to think her life was over, God had given her a way out—the Barley Green, the digestive enzymes, then a chiropractor whose treatments made her no longer need a daily nap.

Perhaps the greatest lesson God taught Elizabeth through all this was about His grace. The apostle Paul's famous line became her constant experience:

My grace is sufficient for you.
2 Corinthians 12:9

She believed this and applied the grace already given her to take her eyes off her pain and focus instead on God and other people. When alone, she would do this by listening to tapes of sermons, studying the Scriptures for hours a day and tuning into Christian radio programs. At night she would listen to sermon tapes through an earpiece, which took her focus off her pain and enabled her to relax and fall asleep. When she was with someone else, she would direct her attention totally to what that person was saying. By re-directing her focus in these ways, her pain ceased to dominate her life and her days were filled with joy. People could SEE God's grace operative in her.

Nevertheless, every day Elizabeth had a choice. The most pain-free place for her was bed, for the more activities she did, the more her body hurt. Yet because she had decided long ago not to develop a pain personality, she would choose not to stay in bed unless she absolutely had to.

"I still have a lot of pain," she says, "but I don't have to dwell on it." The apostle Paul's words made a difference in how she does this:

I have **learned** *to be content*
whatever the circumstances.
Philippians 4:11 (emphasis hers)

"I am learning the same thing," she says. "No matter what situation I'm in, I have to remind myself to choose to be content. It's not what happens to you, but how you respond to it that matters. I can trust God, I know He's in control. Nothing can touch me unless He allows it."

As a nurse, Elizabeth has always enjoyed caring for people. But in all her misfortune, a lot of attention has been focused on her. She now views caring for her eighty-four-year-old mother as an opportunity to be the one who's doing the giving. By pacing herself, Elizabeth is able to do it. "I recall the days when I would lie on the floor in the back of the church," she says. "How far I've come!"

No lines of tension mark her face; her eyes suggest there's a gentle peace within. A soft glow lights her countenance. If Elizabeth doesn't reveal it, no one would have the slightest clue that she lives in constant pain.

* * *

All of us want to have a life of happiness, and we assume that good health is a necessary component of such a life. Surely, a loving and sovereign God would want this for His children. Yet Elizabeth Demkin's story contradicts all that. Why would God allow such a thing?

God is in the business of proclaiming His truth, however He chooses, because when we know the truth, it sets us free (John 8:32). And one of the most powerful ways to make truth real is to illustrate it through a person.

Elizabeth's daily life proclaims several of God's most powerful truths. This woman, living in constant pain, is absolutely certain that God cherishes her and has sovereignly ruled through all her harrowing circumstances, exactly as Scripture says:

> *[He] accomplishes all things*
> *according to the counsel of his will.*
> Ephesians 1:11 RSV

A person watching her can be mystified: If someone like Elizabeth believes God loves us and is in control, surely it

must be true. Of all people, Elizabeth would have sufficient reason to say, "How could God possibly love me,
letting me go through so much trauma? If He does love
me, it's obvious that He doesn't have the power to control
my circumstances." But her convictions about God's love
and His sovereignty often slip into her conversation
because they're so much a part of her personhood.

Elizabeth's life broadcasts the message that Jesus Christ
is worth loving and trusting, regardless of what He does
with and through a person's life. Most people would have
a hard time trusting someone who brought them a great
deal of pain. Yet, amazingly, God takes credit for all of
Elizabeth's pain-producing experiences:

Is it not from the mouth of the Most High
that both calamities and good things come?
Lamentations 3:38

What kind of God is this? He brings her pain and yet has
won her trust and affection. Such inevitable questions in
the hearts of those around her DRAW them into wanting
to know her God more deeply. He must be incredible to
have won her to such a degree.

Elizabeth's life declares what God says about His grace
is absolutely, unalterably, resoundingly true—

My grace is sufficient for thee:
for my strength is made perfect in weakness.
2 Corinthinians 12:9

A person observing her can't help but see this truth at work.
Her soft, sweet demeanor attracts people; she is completely

absorbed in what other people are saying. True, she walks slowly and if you hug her you might feel the metal rod attached to her spine, but she gives no outward indication she's enduring extraordinary pain at that moment. Such is the phenomenon of the living, active grace of God that's available when a person realizes that it's there for the taking.

Elizabeth wordlessly lets everyone know that contentment is possible in trying circumstances. In a world where it's considered normal to complain about financial difficulties or the weather or a bout of flu, Elizabeth walks through her days in a pain-racked body, not just content but joyful.

Countless people come to the end of their lives wondering, *What is my legacy? Am I leaving anything of worth behind me when I die?* They may have lived healthy lives, traveled to exotic destinations, made a lot of money—but none of that can erase the ache of seeing no significant legacy from one's life. Elizabeth never has to consider that, for long, long after she has gone, her life will still be proclaiming God's eternal, liberating truths.

Chapter Sixteen

THE INTERRUPTED CHRISTMAS

Christmas was Betty Meschke's favorite holiday. Ever since childhood her excitement had built as the yearly preparations moved forward—cookie baking with its wonderful smells wafting through the house, the spicy scent of the tree, the colors of the lights and ornaments—all were precious ingredients in the build-up before the big day.

And this year would be even more special, as her parents were

Dave and Betty Meschke with their first two children, five years before this story began.

coming to spend Christmas with her little family—herself, her husband Dave and their three small children. In the days before her mom and dad arrived, they had sent Betty a generous preliminary gift of one hundred dollars. Excitedly, she used it to stock the refrigerator with special treats for the celebration just before they expected her parents to walk in the door.

But on December 23 the whole atmosphere of the holiday changed. Betty will never forget the phone call that forever shattered Christmas for her. Both of her parents were dead, the voice on the phone said. No other vehicle had been involved in the accident. The examining officer explained that her father had probably had a heart attack at the wheel and her parents had been killed instantly. Her father was fifty-eight; her mother fifty-six.

The next day, Christmas Eve, the Meschkes left their own gifts under the unlighted tree and all that wonderful food in the refrigerator, and drove to Bedford, Pennsylvania, where the crash had taken place.

It was Betty's birthday.

She was angry with God—she couldn't help it. Over and over her heart cried out, *Lord, why didn't You let me have my visit with them first and then take them?* She had been so excited about their coming. *Why would the Lord choose to do this when they were so young?*

The wrecked car had carried a bounty of gifts, their wrappings and contents testifying silently to the loving care which Betty's parents had lavished on each present as they looked forward to the time with their precious family. Now the three children silently opened the gifts in a cold, cheerless hotel room. Then the Meschkes drove on to Betty's parents' hometown for the funeral.

As she stood alone in the funeral home, staring at her parents' lifeless bodies, Betty cried out in her heart, *Lord! Give me some comfort!* Suddenly she felt physically warm, as though she were being held in the Lord's arms. But her caustic anger would take a long time to burn itself out.

On December 29, a bitter, snowy day in Chicago, Betty and Dave buried her parents. "I just can't bear to go away and leave them here in this freezing earth," she cried to her husband.

"Honey, they're not here," he assured her, putting his arm around her. "They're with the Lord."

"I know," she wept, "but those are the very bodies that I used to hug!"

Betty knew in her head that her parents were in heaven. She had often heard and believed the Scriptures about the guaranteed future of those who trust in Jesus Christ. Scriptures such as 1 John 5:11-12—

> *God has given us eternal life,*
> *and this life is in his Son.*
> *He who has the Son has life;*
> *he who does not have the Son of God*
> *does not have life.*

Her father had taught her that; her husband had, too. She well knew that a good God was supposed to be in control of everything. However, her Christian beliefs lived mostly in her head and had not penetrated deep within her heart. She found little comfort in knowing that her mom and dad were in heaven.[1] Where was heaven? Nobody could tell

---

[1] See Appendix A to understand how a person can be sure of going to heaven.

her that, and unconsoled, she only wanted them here on earth with her.

Over time her anger subsided but it didn't disappear. It still lurked in the corner of her heart, unconsciously coloring every event in her life.

Eight years later, her Navy chaplain husband was preparing to leave for the battlefields of Vietnam. By now Dave and Betty had five children, ages three to fifteen. Without Dave, Betty knew she'd be alone with much to worry about.

One Sunday just before Dave's departure, two lines in the sermon she heard riveted her: "There is nothing that comes into your life that is a surprise to God. Every single circumstance has gone past His throne and has been approved." As she sat in that pew she thought, *Dave's going to Vietnam has been approved by God. I don't have to like what the Lord has done. I don't have to understand it, either.* Suddenly she recalled the verses that she and Dave had chosen for their lives when they were married:

Trust in the Lord with all your heart
and lean not on your own understanding;
in all your ways acknowledge him,
and he will make your paths straight.
Proverbs 3:5-6

Filled with wonder, she realized that God didn't expect her to understand. *He* understands. He just expected her to trust Him and believe that He knew what He was doing.

God really is in charge, she concluded. *He doesn't make mistakes.* Then, releasing herself slowly into the security of this truth, she could now totally surrender Dave and his safety in war-torn Vietnam to her heavenly Father. And she now felt sure that she and the children would be well taken care of, too.

This realization spilled over onto the long-standing issue of her anger at God for taking her parents so early in their lives. Now she could acknowledge that the fatal accident two days before Christmas had received the Lord's approval before it even took place. She still didn't understand why it had to happen, but at last she could believe that in God's goodness and wisdom He had chosen to let them die on that day in that way.

Suddenly as she believed that a good God was in control of her husband's safety and had made no mistake the day her parents died, her anxiety and anger slipped away. The simple mental act of believing this truth calmed her spirit and gave her a sweet peace.

* * *

The Bible is full of statements that God sits on His throne and rules in the affairs of men. But few Christians internalize that unseen phenomenon and so they walk through life torn by anxiety, fear and anger over inexplicable events that shatter their lives. However, one day years ago one wife believed one truth spoken from one pulpit and ascended to a lofty place reserved for those who decide to believe that the Lord is truly in control and knows what He's doing.

"If we really knew how much God is in control, we would just relax and enjoy the ride," says Dr. Jack Hough. Betty Meschke began relaxing and enjoying the ride as a young mother and her life took on a new dimension of joy. Although she still missed her husband while he was in Vietnam, worry about his safety did not dominate her days or rob her of enjoying her children during his absence.

Years later when the Meschkes' children became teen-agers, one of them often brought Betty to her knees in prayer. However, she always knew deep down that nothing could touch her boy unless her wise Father thought it was a good idea. She stood firm on that certainty and after twelve years that son finally decided that following the Lord was the best way to live.

Now, that view of God on His throne, approving or thwarting whatever is about to occur on earth, calms Betty as she prays for her grandchildren.

Although she would love to have had her parents nearby for many more years, she is astounded at how their death forced her, after an eight-year struggle, to learn to trust God—a lesson that has sweetened every day of her life. For in trusting the Lord on a new level, she grew closer to Him, resulting in a richness that makes other women want to tap into her wisdom. There is a softness and peaceful assurance about her manner that hints to others that this woman feels safe in the shadow of the Almighty.

There is no way Betty could have imagined that when God took her parents He was setting the stage to enable her to receive one of the greatest gifts that God gives—the ability to trust Him when life is hard. She had no idea that this gift would make her a role model for moms who assume that anxiety about the safety of those they love is just part of motherhood. They only have to spend some time getting to know Betty Meschke to find out that even a mother can walk in peace.

Chapter Seventeen

THE STORY OF LI'L JOE

D ana lay quietly in her hospital bed, filled with the tired serenity of a mother who has just given birth. In the nursery down the hall lay tiny Joseph Hamilton Steers, her firstborn, a miracle almost beyond comprehension for both Dana and her husband Tom. She must rest, for soon they would go home.

For the next few weeks, she and Tom had planned to bring Joseph with them to stay at her parents' home. For Dana would need the help and encouragement of her mother in the first days

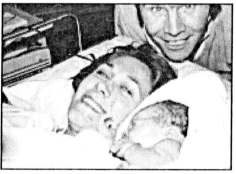

The day Little Joe was born.

of caring for the precious newcomer. Those thrilling days flew by.

Then, one horrible morning just two weeks after he was born, Joseph awoke with a high fever. Frightened, Tom and Dana rushed him back to the hospital where Joe was immediately admitted to the pediatric intensive care unit. The diagnosis? Maybe pneumonia and an infection. "You have a very sick child," the doctor warned them.

Two days later, more bad news awaited them. Little Joseph's liver and spleen had dangerously enlarged. The following day, Christmas Eve, the doctors found that he also had a seriously reduced platelet count, badly compromising his clotting mechanism. "Your son is a time bomb," the hematologist, said. "Any internal or external bruising could be fatal."

The days ground on, a blur of Dana trying to nurse Joe while she and Tom stayed with him as much as possible at the hospital. They took quick breaks to go to her parents' home nearby to take a shower, get some sleep and change their clothes—the only diversion in their endless round of inexpressible concern.

Daily blood samples became a routine in the baby's existence. Except these were not routine blood samplings. Tiny Joe would cry and squirm while the hospital personnel tried to insert just one more needle into his threadlike blood vessels. His veins would collapse from so many needles poking him. The nurses had to look for new veins to draw blood from, even veins around his face.

One day Tom watched a doctor fail three times to penetrate a vein in order to draw a little blood. Nobody could explain to wee Joe what was happening. All he knew was pain and more pain. Anxious, Tom went out into the hallway and helplessly pleaded with God to direct the needle inside a vein. Realizing that his anxiety meant he was not trusting God, Tom started praising the Lord that He would heal Li'l Joe and enable the doctors to acquire the needed blood.

Over the following weeks, Joe's tiny body became badly bloated. The medical staff were mystified by his many symptoms, particularly his swollen internal organs. Joe was kept on intravenous antibiotics to prevent any bacterial infection.

The Steers were on an emotional roller coaster as each new discovery unfolded. The day Joe became sick, Dana had read Psalm 121 in her morning devotions. Tom and Dana clung to that psalm for their baby, especially one verse:

The Lord will keep you from all evil;
he will keep your life.
Psalm 121:7 RSV

The Steers usually led a Bible study on Sunday afternoons for a group of Koreans. Now Tom and Dana asked these Korean friends to come to the hospital to pray. The Steers' pastor also joined them. They anointed small Joseph with oil and asked God to heal him because they believed what God said:

Is any one of you sick?
He should call the elders of the church
to pray over him
and anoint him with oil in the name of the Lord.
And the prayer offered in faith
will make the sick person well;

the Lord will raise him up.
James 5:14-15

Relatives, friends, prayer chains and churches near and far were also praying. On Sunday December 26, at least four churches prayed for Li'l Joe.

"We were wide open for anxiety and unbelief," says Tom. "It encouraged us so much that these people were sharing our burden. It lightened our emotional load and kept us trusting God."

Li'l Joe's liver size then came down from five centimeters to two. No one understood why it had swollen so badly in the first place, for his symptoms didn't match those of any other illness ever recorded. Yet they resembled the symptoms of lymphohistiocystosis, a rare disease often thought to be genetic in origin. On the other hand, some doctors thought he might have a viral infection.

The hematologist called in other specialists from the University of California in Los Angeles to look at Joe, and also called specialists in Europe and Israel to ask their advice. Joe's case was one large question mark, but Tom and Dana persisted in believing that God would heal their son because of Psalm 121:7 and the encouragement of their friends. "We did not waver in our faith," says Dana.

However, the massive doses of antibiotics were eating away at their boy's little intestines. And on Valentine's Day, as his daddy sat beside him, the life ebbed out of Li'l Joe's tiny body. The hospital staff who had fought so hard for his life were visibly grief-stricken. Even some male doctors cried.

Tom could hardly take it in. Optimistic by nature, he had really expected God to turn everything around. In tears he went out into the hallway and pounded the wall. At that point God breathed a stunning truth into his thinking:

The perishable must clothe itself with the imperishable,
and the mortal with immortality.
1 Corinthians 15:53

He went back into the room where the medical staff were still standing around his baby's lifeless body and said, "Little Joseph is with the Lord. He has a new body and is perfectly healed at last!" From then on, he and Dana were able to comfort the medical staff.

The two young parents clung to the Scriptures, and many immutable truths gripped them. For example:

All the days ordained for me
were written in your book
before one of them came to be.
Psalm 139:16

They realized that all of our days are numbered by God—not by medical science, not by diseases, not by doctors and not by circumstances. Joseph had been born on Pearl Harbor Day and had died on Valentine's Day. His lifespan had been exactly seventy days. And that was the exact number of days that God had ordained for him.

"God is totally in control of our conception, our birth, our life and our lifespan," says Dana, pointing to the words that convinced her:

You created my inmost being;
You knit me together in my mother's womb . . . .

My frame was not hidden from you
when I was made in the secret place.
When I was woven together in the depths of the earth,
your eyes saw my unformed body.
Psalm 139:13,15-16

"God knew that Joseph's blood was missing certain elements," she says.

Tom adds, "God's wisdom is infinite, but man's is finite. Medical science couldn't solve Joe's problems. And even our prayers didn't bring temporal healing." He points to Isaiah 55:8 to explain why it was not possible to understand what happened—

"My thoughts are not your thoughts,
neither are your ways my ways,"
declares the Lord.

"The bottom line for me," says Dana, "was whether I was going to trust God. And I cannot trust a God who is not in charge. He has to be sovereign." Jesus' words convinced her that He was:

Are not two sparrows sold for a penny?
Yet not one of them will fall to the ground
apart from the will of your Father.
And even the very hairs of your head are all numbered.
So don't be afraid;
you are worth more than sparrows.
Matthew 10:29-31

In her search for further comfort, Dana read C.S.Lewis'

A Grief Observed. As an English major in college, she had done a project on C. S. Lewis and his writing style. Now as she delved deeper into the message of this book, she felt as if she were processing the tragic event with an old friend. "You observe him grieve as he records his experience in a transparent and unfiltered way," she says. "That meant so much to me. The book was heaven-sent. It was incredibly healing. It gave me permission to feel my pain and sadness."

The Steers realized that Satan's goal is to get believers to curse God and die when they lose something precious to them (Job 1:9,11; 2:9). However, that's not what King David of Israel did three thousand years ago. He also pleaded with God for the life of his sick baby and he also didn't get what he asked for. When his baby died, instead of cursing God, David went to the house of the Lord and worshiped (2 Samuel 12:20).

Tom and Dana chose to follow David's example. Also the king's confidence that he would see his baby again became their conviction as well:

I will go to him,
but he will not return to me.
2 Samuel 12:23

They chose to hold Li'l Joe's memorial service in the hospital chapel so that the medical staff who had cared for him so tenderly could attend. Tom spoke, explaining why he and Dana had such great hope. He said, "We have peace that Joe is in heaven with a new body." And he thanked the staff for their support and their love for their baby.

They then sent out a newsletter to friends and supporters, sharing the truths from God that had comforted them. The letter concluded: "Children are a gift from God. Life is a miracle."

Then the Steers had to return to their apartment in Pasadena and Joe's lovely bedroom with blue and white curtains and a special picture on the wall that Dana had crafted herself. Darling little Joseph had never slept there.

Tom felt numb with grief. But as he awoke each morning with acute pain in his heart, he was overwhelmed by an unanticipated anointing of God's grace. "While we were walking through the valley of the shadow of death, there was this incredible Presence. And even though it was dark, we were walking in light," he says now. Dana, too, had a heart filled with peaceful sorrow. She had wanted a baby son; she had wanted to have lots of boys who could become athletes, as she herself had played football. And Li'l Joe had had such strong-looking, football legs!

Dana and Tom were deluged with cards and letters, some from unexpected sources, including the president of Fuller Seminary where Tom was studying for his master's degree. The man told them that his first son had also died. In fact, the Steers found out that many people had lost a baby. "That comforted us," says Dana. "We were not alone in our grief."

Dana then read Elisabeth Kübler-Ross' book *On Death and Dying*. It talked about the grieving process and the normal feelings involved—denial, anger, bargaining with God, depression and finally acceptance. "I learned that it is normal to have these feelings," says Dana. "It was OK to be mad and to feel like life was gray."

Dana loves beauty in every form, and mountain scenery would thrill her as she noted the many subtle shades of

green in the landscape. But now the world became color-
less, food no longer tasted interesting, life felt like an endless, dreary tunnel. She lost weight and could not bear to
wear colorful clothing, even going so far as to wear a scarf
over her hair tied behind her neck. Her grief stood right
out there for all the world to see.

But as the Steers worked through their pain, comfort
also came to them through Joseph's name itself. Although
they had planned to use only family names for their
children, they both had an inexplicable conviction that this
baby should be named Joseph. Yet no one in either of their
families bore that name.

Now Dana began to study the life of the biblical Joseph,
the first son of Rachel, Jacob's favorite wife. Rachel had
difficulty conceiving, but when she finally had a baby, she
named him Joseph, which means "The Lord will add."
When Dana learned this, the Lord spoke to her heart, *I will
add children to your life.*

After Li'l Joe's death, the doctors had advised the Steers
not to have any more children because it was possible that
their son had had lymphohistiocystosis. "It's a disease
which *seems* to be genetic," they said. "If it is, there is a
high probability that your next child will have it, too."

Encouraged by the meaning of Joseph's name, Dana was
open to having more children despite the doctors' warn-
ings. Tom was enthusiastic. "Hey, the doctors don't know
anything for sure," he told Dana. "But we know God, who
does know everything. So let's put our trust in God, not
the doctors. When God gives you peace and you feel ready,
let's try to have another baby."

Five months after Li'l Joe's death, Dana felt hopeful
again and they decided to go ahead. Within a few weeks,

she became pregnant. "However, I would not have been ready so soon if I hadn't let myself grieve," she says.

Two months later, the Steers took a long trip by car and as they were driving home, Dana began to bleed profusely. As soon as they walked into the house, she called the doctor. "I guess I've lost the baby," she said.

"Come in and let me check you," he replied. They both heard the baby's heartbeat coming strongly through the stethoscope. The doctor was amazed. The baby was alive!

Dana was confined to bed for months, and many days as she lay there she continued to bleed. As the baby grew, so did her anxiety about its health and safety. Even though she had never had acne in her life, not even as a teenager, she now developed a severe case, probably from tension.

Day after day, in her bed, she read the Old Testament. One day she came upon the story of Gideon.[1] God had asked him to lead his people in fighting the Midianites, who would often invade Israel to ravage it. But in Gideon's anxiety over the huge odds against him, he had asked God for a sign that He would be with him. This story encouraged Dana also to ask God for a sign—that the baby in her womb would be healthy and would not have the disease that had killed little Joseph.

Earlier in her Christian life, Dana had been taught that a believer should not ask for special signs from God, as this showed lack of faith. *But Gideon did,* she reassured herself. *He even did it twice.* The biblical passage made it clear that Gideon was a man of little faith. She thought, *Just like me. I'm a woman of little faith. If I had a lot of faith, I wouldn't need a sign. But I need a sign, and that's OK because God meets us where we are.* It was the seventh month of

---

[1] Judges, chapters 6-8.

her pregnancy.

A few weeks later she received an unexpected phone call. Little Joe's hematologist was calling and they had not seen or heard from him in over a year. "A medical researcher recently moved to Los Angeles," he said, "and has studied your baby's records. He's convinced that Li'l Joseph had a virus." He had not died due to a genetic birth defect after all!

God had sent Dana a sign. The hematologist had been under no obligation to call and tell her of the changed diagnosis. Astounded, Dana finished her pregnancy totally at peace, certain that the Lord had spoken through the unexpected phone call.

Then God sent the Steers a second sign. Their baby girl—aptly named Joy—weighed nine and a half pounds. She screamed with such gusto at birth that the nurses commented that they had never seen such a hearty baby. Her neck muscles were so strong that she lifted her head the second day of her life and looked more like a two-month-old than a newborn.

At Joy's first-year checkup, the doctor said she was too small. Her weight was in the bottom ten percent on the growth chart for American babies. "I refused to worry about it," says Dana. "The doctors were worried, but I wasn't."

She turned out to be right. Joy grew up to

The Steers family in 2001.

become a small, vibrant woman, only five feet three inches tall. No wonder she was petite at age one. Dana is convinced that God made her weigh a lot at birth just to reassure Dana of the baby's health and strength.

And then God added more children to the Steers—two more healthy ones, Robert and Anna.

* * *

The years have passed. And now with hindsight Tom and Dana can see that Li'l Joe's tiny lifespan produced a multitude of blessings:

During his seventy days of life his parents had to trust God as they had never trusted Him before. They had to lean on Him for guidance as to what to do with their sick baby. They had to trust Him to enable the doctor to penetrate his veins with a needle. They had to trust God to mend their broken hearts after their boy's death. They had to trust Him with all their questions about why their darling baby died. They had to trust Him to give them healthy children despite the doctors' warning. They had to trust Him to confirm that their second baby in Dana's womb was OK despite profuse bleeding. They had to trust Him that Joy's tiny frame at age one was not a bad sign as the doctor had thought. Thus, trusting God with life's imponderable issues just became a way of life for the Steers—something that others watch and often want to imitate.

While Tom and Dana were still in the stage of raw grief, God was using their confidence in Li'l Joe's destination to comfort the hospital staff who had no assurance of anything good happening after death. They had observed the Steers hurt and pray and struggle. Now the medical team watched two parents who should have been angry, bitter and depressed speak with confidence that Joe's life had taken a dramatic turn for the better. Death is so wrenching, so final, yet this couple emitted hope. The witness of their faith had an incalculable effect on the hospital staff.

Throughout the year that encompassed Joe's life and the Steers' grief, the two parents kept hearing God's voice. God spoke to Dana through Psalm 121 the day Li'l Joe became sick. God spoke to Tom as he pounded his fists on the hospital wall. God spoke to both of them about His sovereignty over the exact length of Joe's life. God spoke to Dana as she read about C.S. Lewis wading through his grief. God spoke to both of them through the meaning of Joseph's name. God spoke to pregnant Dana in her doubts as she, like Gideon, sought a sign because of her small faith.

Thus, they got used to hearing from God often and seeking His answers for whatever came their way. It became a habit. Therefore, their lives for nearly thirty years since Joe died has been illustrating the truth of James 4:8—

Draw near to God
and He will draw near to you.
(New American Standard Bible)

Would they wish that they could get Little Joe back? Of course. Would they want to lose the deep changes God wrought in the core of who they are because they lost their baby? No. Yet in God's economy they will one day get their son back. They will end up getting everything they wanted after all.

Chapter Eighteen

THE WOMAN IN THE MASK

S he sat silently on a bench in the middle of the busy mall. Most passers-by paid no attention to her, but children walk at the height of seated adults and they look at everything. Suddenly a little boy was standing beside her.

"Why are you wearing a mask?" he inquired. "It's not Halloween!"

She smiled at him warmly. "No, it's not Halloween, and this isn't really a mask. It's a special kind of Band-Aid to help my face get better. I was badly burned awhile ago and it's taking a long time to get well, but this bandage will help." Reassured, the child ran after his mother.

"Really, Jeremy, you shouldn't ask people embarrassing questions!" his mother scolded.

But Diane Bringgold much preferred the earnest questions from children to the blunt stares or averted eyes she often received from adults around her.

Although only a few months had passed, it seemed
years since that gray Monday afternoon when her whole
life had abruptly changed. Diane and her family were
returning from a pleasant weekend in the mountains five
hundred miles from their home near Los Angeles. But on
the day they planned to fly home in their small aircraft, the
snow as well as the low clouds made her husband Bruce
decide to wait until the next day when the weather was
predicted to be better.

However, the next morning visibility was still poor, but
by afternoon it was good below the low-hanging clouds,
so Bruce planned to follow the valley to a wider place where
they could fly up through the clouds into the sunshine without fear of hitting a mountain. From there it would be easy
to fly home. But shortly after they took off, the wind broke

Bruce and Diane Bringgold a few years before this story.

up the clouds and they were surrounded by a mass of gray fog. They could see nothing. Then unexpectedly they saw the trees on the side of the mountain and although Bruce turned sharply to avoid hitting the earth head-on, the plane crashed into the butte and everything went black.

As Diane slowly regained consciousness, she heard only the crackling of flames. She could feel her face, hands and feet burning. Bruce's lifeless body lay across hers. He did not move; he made no sound. Pushing him off, she wiggled to get her seatbelt unfastened, slid out the door and crawled away. Immediately the gas tank exploded, and the plane went up in flames.

She could hear Jim and Virginia Dixon, friends who were flying with them, calling for her, but she didn't answer. She hid behind a pile of rocks, longing to die. Her wonderful husband and their three children had perished in the crash. Excruciating pain from severe burns permeated her body. *How can I go on living?* she asked herself. *How long will it take me to die if nobody finds me? If only it were colder so I could freeze to death quickly.*

The next scene was crystal clear in Diane's memory. She had looked up, and about ten feet away she'd seen a man dressed in radiant white. In a firm and compassionate voice He had said, *Diane, it is not up to you to decide whether to live or die. That decision is Mine alone to make.*[1]

She recalled her reaction, one that came almost in spite of herself: *Lord, I can't face being widowed, childless and badly burned . . . . If You want me to live, I will give You my life, but You'll have to cope with my pain, loneliness and grief. I can't.*[2]

---

[1] Bringgold, Diane, *Life Instead* (Ventura, California: Howard Publishing, 1979), p. 18. All quotations from this book are used by permission.
[2] Ibid.

In that moment she sensed such love flowing from Him that she had felt reassured that He would do as she'd asked. Then as suddenly as He'd appeared, He vanished.

Diane could hear cars on the highway below them and Jim and Virginia's voices calling for help. They'd also suffered extensive second and third-degree burns. Finally she called out to let them know she was alive.

Rescuers arrived on the scene and began the delicate task of taking the three victims down the mountainside. The unstable ground brought a new landslide of loose shale at every step. If the rescuers slipped, the victim would plunge down the mountain in the thick fog, so it was necessary to stabilize each stretcher by securing it to rocks and trees as they worked their arduous way to the bottom. Every man was risking his life to bring the three crash victims to safety.

Three hours later, Diane, Jim and Virginia had been moved part way down the mountain to a waiting ambulance. The paramedics wrapped Diane's wounds but her vital signs were so unstable they weren't sure she'd survive the rest of the trip to the health center. But Diane knew she'd survive; the Lord had made it quite clear that He wanted her to live.

The nearest burn unit was about one hundred miles from the crash site. There, the staff wrapped Diane's head, legs and hands in bandages that felt to her like a lovely soft cocoon. Her head soon looked like a large pumpkin and her arms were elevated with slings, while an IV supplied water and nourishment and a catheter removed her body wastes. She would not be allowed to eat or drink anything for a day, making her constantly thirsty.

Although she was given painkillers, she sensed the Lord

protecting her from much of her agony. Despite a compression fracture of her back, it hurt only during x-rays.

The doctor had grave doubts whether he could save her badly damaged right hand, and he made incisions to preserve its deep circulation. Then on the seventh day the medical team grafted new skin onto it and bandaged it, not knowing if the graft would take. People prayed, and when the doctors removed the bandages six days later, her hand looked swollen and purple, with skin like cellophane. To Diane it looked ghastly, but the surgical team thought it looked great although later they did have to do new grafts on the tips of her fingers. Her heart swelled with gratitude that she still had her hand.

All the while that hand felt constantly cold and it ached as if submerged in a bowl of ice water. Twice a day she had physical therapy to help her regain its function. Skin still didn't cover the tips of her fingers and the pain was excruciating when she bent her hand even slightly. Her little finger complained the most, but she told it, *You're too small to hurt so much!* The tip had been burned off to the first joint, so there wasn't a lot of it left to hurt.

Before new skin could be grafted onto any area, the old damaged skin had to be removed. To facilitate the removal, the medical staff would wrap her wounds in wet gauze, and as it dried the dead skin stuck to the bandages. Every six hours they changed these wrappings and as they crept closer and closer to healthy tissue, removing the gauze became more and more painful. So Diane took extra pain medication each time just before her wrappings were removed. If the area bled, this indicated that healthy tissue had been reached and new skin could now be grafted over the raw wounds. In addition, her leg burns had to be scraped with a scalpel and two nurses had to hold her down so she couldn't grab the doctor's arm to make him stop.

Her recovery was amazing. After just a few days the nurses were able to remove her IV and catheter, and ten days after the accident she could use her left hand. *Oh, how wonderful to be able to feed myself!* she thought, *to push a button to call a nurse, to turn the pages of a book.* Although she'd always prided herself on her self-sufficiency, she now had to learn to ask for help and accept it graciously.

Moving the three feet from her bed to the bathroom proved to be a major undertaking, for she had to wear a back brace for the journey. Whenever she put her feet on the floor, her legs would throb horribly as blood flowed into her lower extremities. After the doctor grafted new skin onto her legs, she was delighted to be able finally to take a short and shaky, but pain-free walk with the help of a nurse.

With her head wrapped up in bandages, her hair was filled with dirt, dried blood and medication. After she'd been having sponge baths for two weeks, it took three showers to remove all the dirt and debris from her hair.

Diane experienced pain only during the dressing changes, trips to the bathroom, and physical therapy for her right hand. Otherwise, she was comfortable. She had told the Lord on the mountainside that she couldn't take much pain and, sure enough, He saw to it that she had no more pain than she could handle. That was only one of the problems bombarding her, and with each one she cried out to the Lord. To her amazement she was finding Psalm 34:17 to be literally true:

> *The righteous cry out*
> *and the Lord hears them;*

he delivers them from all their troubles.[3]

Removing the dead skin from her fingertips had to be done with tweezers. Although Diane had previously been too squeamish even to remove splinters from her children's fingers, she now took over this task herself because she could then stop for a rest when the pain was becoming too great. *The Lord is giving me strength to perform any task He deems necessary,* she marveled.

Until new skin was grafted onto the burned areas of her hands, face and legs, her body demanded a great deal of extra energy for the healing process. Burn victims usually need to consume three times as many calories as other patients, and Diane had such a craving for food that even the hospital food tasted good to her.

Providentially, her husband's two business partners handled her family's funeral arrangements at the Bringgolds' Episcopal church. The four caskets starkly emphasized the magnitude of the tragedy. During the time of the service, Diane sat in her hospital bed, reading the funeral liturgy from the *Book of Common Prayer,* while her heart was far away at the service for her precious family.

People later described for her how beautiful and dignified the funeral had been. Friends, including some of her children's playmates, had filled the church. One of the pallbearers had described Bruce as "a guy who brought a lot of joy into a lot of people's lives." It eased Diane's pain to see how many people shared her grief.

---

[3] This promise is for "the righteous" which in Scripture refers to someone who has been imputed as righteous because he puts his trust in Jesus, the Messiah, the only truly righteous One. It also implies that, as a result, that person strives to obey God, but it doesn't mean he does so perfectly.

Bill Peck, one of Bruce's business partners, had dreaded visiting her, for he expected her to say, "Bill, I don't want to live. I have nothing to live for." As he entered her hospital room, he held her by her shoulders and said in his most comforting voice, "Everything is going to be all right." To his astonishment, she replied, "I know it will, Bill." He left the room, relieved and astonished.

Immediately after the crash, God began to bring good out of the tragedy by mending Diane's relationship with her sister JoAnn. Born three years after Diane, JoAnn nevertheless grew to be six inches taller. So people expected her to be able to do everything Diane could, creating conflict and resentment between the two. Now, JoAnn's husband urged his wife to go serve her sister over one hundred miles away. For the first five weeks after the crash he and his family cared for themselves for Diane's sake, while JoAnn kept her sister's loneliness at bay, fed her when both hands remained bandaged, and served her in countless ways. During that time, Diane discovered a compassionate and capable side to JoAnn that she'd never known before.

The headlines throughout the community were full of the tragedy, triggering prayers and concern from many people. Diane received three hundred cards and letters. It deeply touched her that so many people cared enough to write. In the past, she herself had held back from writing notes to sick people because she didn't know what to say. Now she realized that all someone needed to do was write the words "I care" on a blank sheet of paper and mail it.

Many letters mentioned the constant phone calls flowing between the Bringgolds' hometown of Ventura five hundred miles away, and Chico where Diane, Virginia and Jim lay in the hospital. One nurse kept busy almost full time for two days after they arrived, answering the phone to give the latest updates on the condition of the three crash survivors. Whenever Diane felt like giving up, she'd think of the hundreds of people who'd showed her that they cared. She just couldn't let them down.

Many people wanted to help, and Diane gave all of them tasks to do: JoAnn wrote thank-you notes. Other friends at home sent expressions of gratitude to the rescue crew. One person took her dog home and someone else fed the cats. Still others cleaned out the Thanksgiving leftovers in her refrigerator. "People do respond when they know there's a need," she says. "Unfortunately, many of us try so hard to handle our own problems . . . we don't even allow our friends the privilege of sharing our burdens."[4]

Diane knew full well that she herself didn't have the strength to cope with her tragedy, but she was trusting God to sustain her. At night alone, her tears would flow. She was irked at people who viewed her as a strong person, but then realized she encouraged that impression by always putting on a happy face. She was just trying to let her grieving friends and family know that she'd be all right.

Diane's injuries were so extensive that it took all the strength she could muster to concentrate on her own recovery. She simply had no energy left to weep over the deaths of her loved ones. By the time she was strong enough to grieve and fully grasp the extent of her loss, that loss had slowly become a part of her, and the shock of her family's death was not nearly so great as it would have been had she come out of the accident unharmed.

Whenever she cried, her tears made her head bandages wet. Lying in damp bandages for several hours until the

---

[4] Ibid., p. 47.

hospital staff could change them was most uncomfortable, so she would make herself postpone crying until just before the nurse came to change the old gauze for new. Often by then a visitor or a stack of letters or a Bible verse had lifted her spirits and she didn't feel like crying anymore.

Of course, her primary concern for her family was: *Where are they now?* The old familiar verse, John 3:16, put her heart totally at rest about them:

> *For God so loved the world*
> *that He gave His one and only Son*
> *that whoever believes in Him shall not perish,*
> *but have eternal life.*

She knew that her husband and children had put their trust in Jesus, and these words from Christ Himself assured her that her loved ones now lived in heaven. In spite of this wonderful comfort, in the middle of the night she would cry out, "Why me, Lord? Why did You have to take my wonderful family? I loved them so much!"

Christian death is not the worst thing that can happen, Diane, the Lord whispered softly to her heart. *In fact, death is the perfect healing. There is no pain and suffering in heaven.*

"But why couldn't they have lived?" she asked in tears.

Diane, would you really want them to be alive even if they were suffering, if they were permanently disabled or if they had brain damage? Wouldn't you rather have the assurance that they were in heaven with Me? . . . Are you not being selfish when you fail to rejoice for them?[5]

Suddenly she realized that she was grieving for herself, not for her precious loved ones, sad that they no longer

---

[5] Ibid., p. 50.

would give her pleasure. But she could rejoice that they were now with the Lord. She also saw that if just Bruce or one of the children had not died, they would have suffered a great deal. Bruce, her college sweetheart, had valued his family above his law practice. It would have been very difficult for him to deal with his sense of guilt if all the children had died or if he had had to watch his wife suffer. Although he didn't cause the accident, he could well have blamed himself for the rest of his life.

At first, Diane was angry at Bruce, even though they had both believed it was safe to take off that afternoon in the plane. She needed to blame someone and letting herself feel this anger toward him for awhile helped her cope.

That freed her to grieve the loss of her children first. They had all felt so close to each other, and the entire family enjoyed a special bond. Gradually Diane actually came to the point that she was glad none of the children had had to deal with losing each other or one of their parents. After she'd resolved the painful issue of no longer having her children with her, she was then able to release her anger toward Bruce and grieve for him as well.

A few weeks after the accident, Christmas arrived. Seeing little ones in toy ads on television reminded Diane of her own children, and her tears would well up. But Christmas also brought her joy because it reminded her that Jesus had come to live and die to take the punishment for the sins of those who put their trust in Him.[6] Because He came, her family was living in heaven at that very moment.

Diane also realized that God could empathize with her. He had experienced what it felt like to lose a child. Although He knew that Jesus would conquer death and rise again,

---

[6] See Appendix A to understand why this is true.

Still He must have grieved for Him,[7] Diane thought. *God can feel my pain!*

Then she understood that God experiences a far worse pain than hers—rejection by His children, and He feels that pain every day. *His grief over His lost children makes my grief insignificant,* she thought.[8]

Diane saw God using different people to meet her varying needs. The hospital staff helped promote her physical healing, her friends eased her loneliness, and God Himself was healing her great grief. An Episcopal priest visited her. Only thirty years old, he had never seen anyone face a tragedy of this dimension. "I want to assure you that God is with you," he said. Her reply stunned him: "Yes, I know." As he continued to visit her he realized that God's love and grace can actually meet every human need, for Diane's life vividly illustrated that amazing truth.

Until now, Diane had kept her greatest secret to herself—that Jesus had appeared to her in person on the mountain to comfort her. *People will just think I was hallucinating,* she thought. *I don't want anyone worrying that I'm losing my mind.* Finally she decided to confide in the Episcopal priest, and to her grateful surprise, he believed her.

She was discovering that Satan's primary weapon is doubt. He wanted her to question the miracle she'd experienced. *You didn't really see Jesus,* he'd whisper. *You just imagined it.* But the gift of faith that God had given her the night of the crash and the way He'd answered so many prayers since then made it impossible for her to doubt that the vision had actually happened.

---

[7] Ibid., p. 53.

[8] Ibid.

Dr. Richard Morgan, her Christian plastic surgeon, consistently undergirded Diane with emotional support, seeking positive ways to help her face the unpleasant journey of convalescence ahead of her. A month after the plane crash he suggested she go to the beauty parlor, even though it seemed senseless to have her hair done, only to have it wrapped in bandages again. But he hoped in this way to lessen the shock when she saw her face in the mirror for the first time since the accident. He himself removed her bandages in the beauty parlor as they looked in the mirror. Diane was amazed at how good she appeared, and her thrilled surprise relieved him.

Two weeks later he encouraged her to move from the hospital to the nearby Holiday Inn. In that way, she could still return for her daily therapy sessions but would no longer be restricted by the hospital routine. Two friends came from her hometown to help her move and to shop for clothes that would fit over her back brace. She walked out into the real world with a ponytail sticking out of the top of her bandaged head, exhilarated to be free.

But the first night at the Holiday Inn became a fog of loneliness when her two friends left her room. She'd never slept alone in a motel room before. Just as she was beginning to feel the pain of her loss, Dr. Morgan called, thinking she might be lonely.

"I love the freedom of being out of the hospital," she reassured him, "but in some ways I like the hospital better because you people waited on me hand and foot."

"That's one reason I thought you should leave," he said.

The next day her two friends returned home, but Jim and Virginia Dixon, who had also been injured in the crash, were staying in the room next to Diane's, so she wasn't totally abandoned. She continued to blame herself for the Dixons' suffering, for she was the one who'd invited them to fly home with her family. However, no word of blame ever came from either of their mouths. Now every morning Virginia visited Diane to help her dress and open the motel room door, which required one hand to turn the key and another to pull the door open. *The Lord is still teaching me to accept help graciously,* she thought.

Virginia also faced the world with her head wrapped in bandages. She looked like a nun with her face peeking out. But in Diane's case, only her eyes, the tip of her nose and her mouth showed through small openings in her bandages. She dreaded other people's reactions to her strange appearance, but most people treated her with consideration and sympathy because they could see that she had been badly injured.

Two years before the crash a new procedure for greatly reducing burn scars had been developed—wearing tight elastic clothing called Jobst garments. The constant pressure from these garments significantly minimizes the normal contraction of skin undergoing healing. A few weeks after she left the hospital, Diane received her own Jobst garments. One resembled a tight ski mask to be worn over her head, day and night, with only her eyes, nose, mouth and ears showing. An unexpected boon from this unsightly headgear was that she no longer had to fuss over her makeup and hair.

But she looked like a Martian, and if she put on a scarf and tied it in back, she looked like a bank robber. One day when she entered a savings and loan company, the manager almost pushed the emergency button before he realized that she was a customer. Later, at a drive-through

Diane Bringgold, three months after the accident.

fast-food restaurant, the girl behind the cashier's window threw up her hands as if Diane were a gun-toting bandit.

Further discomfort came from her other Jobst clothing—gloves, a tight vest, and toeless pantyhose. These garments covered every square inch of skin where the flames had burned her or where skin had been removed for grafting. The pressure of these garments would help her skin heal smoothly and prevent ugly scarring. During meals she could remove her mask, and in the daytime her left hand didn't need its glove. But at night she felt like she was sleeping in a full-body girdle. At first the sensation was so unpleasant that she needed sleeping pills to doze off.

After Diane returned home to Ventura, she had to walk past a high school on the way to the hospital for her daily therapy sessions. She heard a group of teenaged girls saying, "Did you see that lady in the mask? I'll bet she's really vain. Imagine wearing a mask just to protect your skin!"[9]

Before the plane crash, looking attractive had always been important to Diane. She had never really believed that a person's inner beauty was more significant, as people often insisted. When she was recognized for doing something well, she had always suspected her good looks had

---

[9] Ibid., p. 90.

played a big part in her success. Now she discovered she could succeed in her efforts without her previous beauty, and this freeing discovery made her grateful for her scars. She even came to the point where she rarely thought about her disfigured face and hands. However, Diane still believed that a person should always attempt to look her best, but now she came to see that her own feelings about herself played a more significant role than her looks.

Diane was now a woman alone for the first time in years, and she kept battling bouts of loneliness in that motel room and even after she returned home. *Lord, on the mountainside You promised to help me cope with loneliness. Help!* she'd pray.[10] Invariably, the phone would soon ring.

But it was different when she woke up in the early hours of the morning, before others were awake. At those times she could sense God's presence dissipating her loneliness. It was as if He were in the room, holding her and saying, *It's all right, Diane, you aren't alone. I'm here.*[11] She was awed that God sent the same Holy Spirit to be with her as He had sent to the Christians after Jesus ascended into heaven.

Much of God's comfort came to Diane through other people. Her mother turned out to be a major inspiration. She had been widowed twice and her fortitude gave Diane strength to deal with the loss of her own husband. While she had lost both her partner and her children, her mother had lost three grandchildren and her son-in-law, and her daughter now faced life badly scarred. But the two women were able to comfort one another and reassure each other that the future still had much in store for them.[12]

---

[10] Ibid., p. 59.
[11] Ibid.
[12] Ibid., p. 63.

Two months after the tragedy, Dr. Morgan let Diane return home, but for only four days, as he feared the emotional impact she would face there. She flew home to Ventura in a small plane, unafraid, for she knew it had been the bad weather, not the small aircraft, that had caused the accident.

When she arrived, she went from room to room soaking in the familiar surroundings. She paused to look at the children's school pictures hanging on the wall and thought how fortunate she'd been to have such good-looking kids.[13] Then, obeying Dr. Morgan's strict instructions to call him as soon as she walked into the house, Diane dialed his number. "How great it feels to be home!" she exclaimed.

"Who is with you?" he asked.

"I'm alone."

"I'm not sure I like that."

"The house isn't haunted," Diane reassured him. "It's full of good memories."

Dr. Morgan couldn't believe Diane and later quizzed Bruce's business partners to learn how the weekend had really gone. In fact, her first night in the Holiday Inn had been far lonelier that these few days at home, for here her memories sustained her. Her strong sense of gratitude for the joyful years she'd shared with Bruce and the children overcame her grief. She rejoiced that her children's short lives had been full of joy rather than pain and suffering. She knew it was the Lord who filled her heart with such thankfulness.[14]

Shortly thereafter, she was able to return home for good. The house didn't even feel empty, for her dog and four cats

---

[13] Ibid., p. 69.

[14] Ibid., p. 71.

welcomed her. Then Diane returned to her church. Children surrounded her, asking, "Are you all right?" This woman who had just lost her husband and children made a monumental discovery—the joy of being part of God's family. She joined a prayer group and saw unusual answers to prayer. For example, one woman received a letter from her daughter after fourteen years of silence. Diane would go to church each Sunday just to remind herself that she was part of a wonderful family.[15]

Diane's neighbors often invited her for a meal and made her feel watched over and cared for. She also returned to the organizations she'd belonged to and found she still enjoyed them. When she went for physical therapy, the people there surrounded her with love.

Ten days after her return home, a couple invited Diane to a dance to raise money for the community hospital. She bought a gown that would cover her Jobst underwear, but went without her mask that evening, for she could take it off for special occasions. Other women shared their husbands with her and she danced all night. Although other widows complained of feeling like a fifth wheel in a world of couples, Diane didn't experience that, for people went out of their way to include her in their activities.

The day came when she had to face the task of sorting through her family's belongings, deciding what to keep and what to give away. Memories flooded her mind as she went through her children's possessions. Tears rolled down her cheeks, but they were tears of healing.

She sifted through her husband's treasures—awards he'd won, music he'd written as a boy, a gold coin his grandfather had given him. *Bruce's line has ended*, she thought

---

[15] Ibid., p. 81.

and bitter tears welled up in her eyes. *Why, Lord? Why?* she cried. *Please heal my grief and give me peace again.* Then she recalled that Bruce's sister had children; they were Bruce's line. So she decided to give these precious belongings to them and her peace returned.

Initially, she would look in the mirror, fall back on her bed and cry. *Lord, I don't want to be ugly. I want to look just as I did before,* she would pray. But once she'd poured out her feelings, she could thank God for the marvelous lessons she was learning. She could be grateful to Him for teaching her that she was loved just for herself.[16]

The first time she drove from Ventura to the Chico hospital, she went alone. The drive reminded her vividly of an earlier trip in the car with her two daughters, and memories of her girls came rushing back. Driving along, her eyes filled with tears and she turned off the road to let them flow. Once she had finished crying, she thanked the Lord for her wonderful memories of Mary and Laura. Again He blessed her heart with joy that they hadn't known pain and suffering, and she rejoiced that they were now with Him.[17] She remembered Jesus' words—

Blessed are those who mourn
for they will be comforted.
Matthew 5:4

And she was.

During this time Psalm 30 became one of Diane's favorites for it exactly described what she was going through:

---

[16] Ibid., pp. 92-93.
[17] Ibid., p. 101.

O Lord my God, I cried to Thee for help,
and Thou didst heal me.
Weeping may last for the night,
But a shout of joy comes in the morning.
Thou hast turned for me my mourning into dancing.
Psalm 30:2, 5b, 11a NASB

Diane had come to know Christ in a personal way before she married Bruce. But at the time she didn't want to let God take control of her life for fear of what He might ask her to do. She tried to live as a Christian by her own power, feeling she should be self-reliant and that she should ask for help only as a last resort.[18] But now she *had* to rely on God and other people. In the hospital her desperate straits drove her to read the Bible systematically and she was amazed to watch God lead her to just the right verse when she needed comfort. Now back at home she joined a Bible study group and discovered even more the vitality of God's Word.

It became Diane's habit, when she was discouraged, to ask God to lead her to Scripture that would answer her need. During one low point He led her to Isaiah 26:3—

Thou wilt keep him in perfect peace,
whose mind is stayed on thee.
King James Version

At once she realized, *The reason I don't have peace right now is because my eyes are not on the Lord, but on me.* As she asked Him to help her focus on Him, her peace returned and her grateful heart surprised her.

---

[18] Ibid., p. 14.

She loved watching how the Lord ordered her daily circumstances. One day she couldn't find her car keys as she prepared to leave for her therapy session at the hospital. After a prolonged search she resorted to taking an old car in the garage, which, amazingly, she was able to start. But she was thirty minutes late to her appointment and walked out of her therapy session much later than usual. There she ran into Angela, a member of the prayer group at church. Angela's husband had just had a heart attack and she'd brought him to the hospital. She badly needed someone to be with her and now Diane could be that person.

When she arrived at home, there lay her car keys in the middle of the kitchen floor. Surely she'd have seen them if they'd been there before. Obviously, God had detained her so that she could be at the hospital when Angela arrived.

As time passed, Diane repeatedly recognized God's hand protecting her from pain, easing her loneliness and healing her grief, just as He had promised on the mountainside. "I found the peace and the joy I was experiencing as I continued to walk in God's presence almost indescribable," she says. "I developed an irresistible desire to share what the Lord had done in my life."[19]

However, speaking out boldly had never been natural for her. She was the kind who would hold back her opinions in situations where people might disagree with her and public speaking had always terrified her.

Then a blind reporter wrote a story about Diane that covered the entire first page of the People Section of the local paper. Invitations to speak began to pour in. Finally, she reached a point where she could no longer keep silent— first sharing for just ten minutes at church, then at a

---

[19] Ibid., p. 108.

neighborhood coffee.

Guideposts Magazine wrote a lead story about her, and many readers wrote that the peace and joy on her face in the cover photograph inspired them. Letters filled her mailbox, telling how her story lifted their spirits or how they also had visions of the Lord. Other readers who wrote Diane asked her to write a friend or relative who had faced a tragedy. Diane answered every letter.

Then *The 700 Club* interviewed her for their television show. Every time a new opportunity came, Diane leaned hard on the Lord and went forward. Her mind remained calm but her stomach revealed how panicked she really felt. Seeing herself as just an ordinary person, she knew that without the Lord's constant presence she'd be tongue-tied.[20]

Time and again God would use her to encourage someone. One day she met a man, severely burned in a pulp mill explosion, who'd just begun to wear his Jobst mask. As they talked, he thought, *If she can do it, so can I* —and he persevered in wearing it for two years.

Every night Diane read the obituaries in the newspaper. If someone had lost a husband or child, she wrote to that person and said, "I, too, have lost a husband/child and I know how you feel. I'm praying that God will comfort you." She also told them to call her if they needed a sympathetic ear or a shoulder to cry on. Some responded to her offer. Sharing their pain with her, knowing that she understood it, helped their healing. Just as God had comforted her, she rejoiced when God used her to comfort others. Sometimes she received the joy of a grieving person becoming an ongoing friend.

---

[20] Ibid., p. 118.

As Diane's body healed, she had to struggle through her concerns about how people would react to various ways she would always be disfigured. Although her grafted skin looked pretty normal, a raised purple line emerged along the edges of the grafts on her legs. Those scars made her particularly self-conscious whenever she joined friends to go swimming, but she discovered that the scars didn't show much underwater.

Then there was the issue of her badly damaged right hand—something she could not exactly hide from the public. She had lost the last two joints of her little finger, one joint of her ring finger and the nails and tips of her first and second fingers. Only her thumb looked normal. However, no one even seemed to notice the abnormalities. She discovered that people see what they expect to see. Furthermore, it was hard to feel bad about it because she felt so grateful to have her hand actually functioning as it was supposed to.

A big test of her victory over self-pity came on the first Fourth of July after the plane crash, when Diane visited friends who had often invited her family to stay in one of their cabins over the holiday. On the evening of the Fourth, children ran around the lawn, waving their sparklers. Diane recalled her own children doing that very thing just one year before and even remembered the clothes they'd worn that night. Suddenly the Lord delighted her heart because her children had had such a wonderful experience with their friends. Her heart was not heavy but filled with joy and peace.

When she felt deprived because she no longer had her son and daughters, the Lord invariably led her to visit someone struggling with difficult and demanding children. *There*

ARE advantages on both sides of the fence, she would think. And as she watched friends go through the pain of rejection by their teenage children, she would think, *Surely this is more painful than losing your kids by death. God also had a Son who died. But God suffers more than I do today, for He has many children who have rejected Him.*

Since birthdays and holidays made Diane feel more vulnerable, she asked people to pray that God would turn her pain into joy and protect her from grief especially on those days. She also made sure that she never spent holidays alone. She took special delight in Christmas and Easter, for they reminded her that death is not the end. "If I believed that death were the end, I wouldn't be able to overcome my grief," she'd tell people. She rejoiced that Bruce, Scott, Mary and Laura were all experiencing life in heaven together, now. She did miss them but she was thankful for the many wonderful holidays they had all had together. The joy and gratitude she felt as she celebrated Christmas and Easter couldn't be expressed.

"December 1, 1975—the day of the plane crash—was the end of a wonderful life," says Diane. "I wish I had fully yielded myself to the Lord before that momentous day. But December 1, 1975 was also the beginning of a new life—a wonderful and exciting life in the Lord."[21]

* * *

No one in his right mind would wish that someone would lose his whole family in one tragic instant. Yet Diane's life was immensely enriched through that horrendous experience. Her walk with the Lord had been

---

[21] Ibid., p. 127.

shallow and hardly life-changing before, but after the accident she discovered the thrill of God speaking directly to her need, of trusting Him when no one else could help her, of seeing Him respond to her silent cries for help.

In a place where self-pity and loneliness could have eaten her alive, she experienced God's Spirit personally comforting her. Furthermore, He moved one individual after another to extend himself to her, making her feel popular and cared for, not alone and lonely as would be expected.

In the loss of her family, she made the great discovery that God's family is a real family that shows its love with hugs and thoughtfulness and practical good deeds.

In a world where death and pain are constant factors, Diane became an agent of comfort to friends and even total strangers as she wrote to family members of those she read about in obituaries. She could not withhold the wellspring of comfort that God had been giving her. The shy woman stepped out, trusting God to squelch her fears, and filled speaking engagements. In each of these situations she lived out what Jesus declared to be His desire for every believer:

You are the light of the world.
Matthew 5:14

Thus, she discovered the privilege and exciting adventure of being a beacon in this dark world.

In addition, Diane discovered a great truth—that inner beauty really has significant impact, freeing her from a lie that once had held this beautiful woman captive.

Diane Bringgold's journey from the day she rolled out of a burning plane until now has proved the truth of Jesus' words:

Blessed are the poor in spirit,
for theirs is the kingdom of heaven.
Matthew 5:3

Who could be poorer in spirit than someone lying in the
snow on the side of a
mountain, hoping to die
because she could not face
life with burn scars and no
husband or children? Yet
in her tragedy she found
heaven to be a real place
where her loved ones live
. . . and she found that living in God's presence
does actually bring a large
piece of heaven to earth.

The woman whom
thousands felt sorry for
has become a woman
whose inner beauty most
people would envy.

Diane today.

Note: In 1986 Diane married Don Brown, and ten years later Don was
ordained an an Episcopal priest. They live in Jamestown, North
Dakota. This story is told in full in the book *Life Instead* by Diane
Bringgold, available at Grace Church, 405 Second Ave. N.E., Jamestown,
ND, phone (701) 252-4499.

God Knows What He's About

When God wants to drill a man
      And thrill a man
      And skill a man;
When God wants to mold a man
      To play the noblest part;
When He yearns with all His heart
      To create so great and bold a man
That all the world shall be amazed—
      Watch His methods, watch His ways!
How He ruthlessly perfects
      Whom He royally elects!
How He hammers him and hurts him,
      And with mighty blows converts him
Into trial shapes of clay
      Which only God can understand,
While his tortured heart is crying
      And he lifts beseeching hands!
How He bends, but never breaks
      When his good He undertakes;
How He uses whom He chooses
      And with every purpose fuses him,
By every act induces him
      To try His splendor out—
God knows what He's about!

—J. Oswald Sanders' *Spiritual Leadership*, page 141.

The Christian's Secret Formula

A common denominator in nearly every story in this book is that the main characters have confidence in God and joy in connecting with Him. Here's their secret: The turning point for each of them was when they encountered a body of dynamic information which has attained a specific title—the Gospel.

The life-altering facts of the Gospel are these: God loves us intensely, and He wants to enjoy a sweet, close, conversational relationship with everyone He has made. However, because He is holy, the ugly things we do that emanate from the dark side in all of us offend Him and push Him away from us. We have not lived the life-giving way He intended for us to live. Our consciences tell us that.

When I was a child, my father kept the month's allowances for me and my four siblings in an old Band-Aid can in the top drawer of his dresser. One day I needed change for a dollar, and my mother said I could get it out of the allowance can. In the process of getting the change, I stole ten cents. Would you believe that this little act of thievery bothered me for decades! Finally, when I was thirty-two, I called my father and admitted what I had done, asking him to forgive me. Then, at last, my conscience could rest.

I had violated one of God's standards. I could not escape the guilt I felt, nor would the years erase it.

What then are the standards that this holy God holds us responsible to maintain? They are called the Ten Commandments. Let's see how you'd do if God called you to account today:

Have you ever lied? Well, one commandment is "You shall not give false testimony."

Have you ever stolen something, even something small, like ten cents out of an allowance can? Another commandment states "You shall not steal."

Have you ever hated someone? Jesus considered hate equal to murder, and one of the commandments says "You shall not murder."

Have you ever lusted after someone of the opposite sex? Jesus says that such thoughts make you an adulterer in your heart, and one of the commandments warns "You shall not commit adultery."

That's only four of them. If you have broken even one of these, you are in trouble, for Jesus' half brother James said:

Whoever keeps the whole law
and yet stumbles at just one point
is guilty of breaking all of it.
James 2:10

Most of us expect to live a long time. However, do you think it's possible that you could die today? Of course, and if you did die today and appeared before God, do you think, judging by His standard of the Ten Commandments, you'd go to heaven or hell? Most people think they'd go to heaven, no matter what they've done, because God is loving and merciful. They are right—and they are wrong:

The Lord is slow to anger,
abounding in love
and forgiving sin and rebellion.

Yet he does not leave the guilty unpunished.
Numbers 14:18 (emphasis mine)

Now, let's take a brief detour. Do you know why Jesus Christ died on the cross? Take a moment to think about it. He died to take the punishment that you and I deserve for all the bad things we've done, for all the commandments we've broken. I myself can take the punishment that I deserve—or I can accept what Jesus has done for me.

Let me illustrate. Suppose you and I are riding down one of California's freeways, talking and laughing and having a good time. I'm driving, and because I'm distracted by the pleasure of our conversation, I don't notice that I'm driving too fast.

Suddenly I hear a siren and see a whirling red light in my rearview mirror. A police car is pursuing us, so I pull over to the side of the road.

"Lady, do you know how fast you were going?" the officer asks. And after some conversation, he tells me that I must pay him fifty dollars. As I reach into my purse for the money, you say to me, "Carrie, here, let me pay for it. I was making you laugh and distracted you from concentrating on driving."

"No! No!" I say. "I'll pay. It's my fault."

You shove fifty dollars into my hand, but I resist your gracious act.

Now does the officer care whose fifty dollars he gets? No. He just wants justice to be done. The fine for exceeding the speed limit in that area is fifty dollars. You can pay, or I can pay. Either way, justice is satisfied.

The same is true of the ultimate punishment we all deserve for the wrong way we have lived life. I can take my own punishment from God, or I can accept the punishment that Jesus took for me.

Now how do we obtain this gift of Jesus, and rescue ourselves from the punishment that we should receive? Jesus said:

Unless you repent,
you . . . will all perish.
Luke 13:5

We have broken His commandments. We have not cared about His standards. We have all gone off and lived our lives independently of Him. That's what we need to repent of.

When Jesus died, He confounded everyone by rising from the dead three days later. Forty days after that, He ascended into heaven in full view of His closest followers. He is alive today, and He beckons you to repent and put your trust in Him. A simple prayer to Jesus, that's all it takes to express your sorrow for going against His ways and to tell Him you want to rely Him in life now.

If you do that, God will then credit to your account the punishment that Jesus took for all the bad things that you have ever done. God will declare you clean because Someone else took your punishment. Then when you die—whether it's today or forty years from now—you can walk right into heaven. Here's how you can be sure:

God has given us eternal life,
and this life is in his Son.
He who has the Son has life;
he who does not have the Son of God
does not have life.
1 John 5:11-12

That's the secret of the main characters in all these stories. They've turned their lives over to Jesus Christ, in repentance for the way they've lived before, and they've endeavored to follow Him. Walking with the Prince of Peace gives peace in every area of life. And drinking from the Fountain of Life-Giving Water refreshes:

They have forsaken me,
the Fountain of Life-giving Water;
and they have built for themselves
broken cisterns that can't hold water.
Jeremiah 2:13 LB

Until you take this step of repentance, and entrust your life into the hands of Jesus Christ, you are in great danger. You are just one car accident away from having your next residence determined for all eternity.

Repent and choose Jesus, the Bread of Life, the Light of the World—and embark on the ultimate adventure that life offers.

Index

vision (cont'd):
  of someone dead 50

W

Waruiru, Esther 169–178
water, search for 30–45
wealth, pursuit of 54–66

This is a book about how to charge off into the battle with vigor without killing the horse that carries you there.

What People Say about
Weary Warriors by Carrie Coffman

"This book could save your health and your ministry."
—Jim and Jeri White, The Navigators.

"I am thrilled by this book." —Jim Craddock, president, Association of Biblical Counselors (1987-1998).

"Every missionary should read this book."
—Debi Sayer, Arab World Ministries.

"Stimulating." —Dr. Debbie Aho, missionary counselor.

"Compelling." —Dr. Dan Allender, psychologist.

"Outstanding." —Rev. Ken Royer, pastor to missionaries.

"Tremendous insight." —Greg Lillestrand, Campus Crusade.

Cost: $13.95. Use order form in back of book.

Here's what people say about
Bored Readers Don't Pray Much
by Carrie Coffman

"This book can revolutionize missionary letters."
—Dr. Roger Greenway, Calvin Seminary.

"If you could use some coaching on how to turn out news-letters that capture and hold people's attention, buying this book is one of the best investments you could make."
—*Evangelical Missions Quarterly.*

"I tried out [the principles] in my last newsletter. Friends called me and said they would pray for the person in my story. I got more money [for my ministry], and I didn't even ask for it. **It works! It works!**"
—Alison English, Church Resource Ministries.

"I have long moaned and groaned over the exceedingly boring prayer-letters we receive and wondered if ours were equally boring. Now, here is a book giving us power-ful tools for our prayer-letters. **This book should set prayer warriors ablaze all over the world** as they start getting really effective newsletters from their missionaries."
—Sharon Reeece, Wycliffe Bible Translators in Brazil.

To get people to pray, first you have got to get them interested.

"The book is fantastic. I am struggling to put it down."
—Jane Denyer, JAARS.

Cost: $15. Use order form in back of book.

Majesty Publishers

Quick Order Form

Fax orders: 1-703-669-6738. Send this form.

Telephone orders: 1-703-669-6737 Have credit card ready.

Internet orders: Go to www.majestypublishers.com.

Postal orders: Majesty Publishers, P.O. Box 1623, Leesburg, VA 20177, USA.

Questions: E-mail us at majestypub@adelphia.net.

Please indicate quantity wanted of the following books (satisfaction guaranteed or else the cost of books is returned):

_____ *Sweet Fire* @ $19.95
_____ *Weary Warriors* @ $13.95
_____ *Bored Readers Don't Pray Much* @ $15.00

Name_____

Address_____

City _____State _____ Zip _____-____

Telephone _____

E-mail address _____

Sales Tax: Please add 4.25% for orders sent to Virginia.

Postage & handling: 1 book - $3, 2-3 books - $4, 4-5 books -$6

Payment: (circle which one): check, credit card—Visa or MasterCard

Card number: _____Exp. date: ___/___

Name on card: _____

Majesty Publishers

Quick Order Form

Fax orders: 1-703-669-6738. Send this form.

Telephone orders: 1-703-669-6737 Have credit card ready.

Internet orders: Go to www.majestypublishers.com.

Postal orders: Majesty Publishers, P.O. Box 1623, Leesburg, VA 20177, USA.

Questions: E-mail us at majestypub@adelphia.net.

Please indicate quantity wanted of the following books (satisfaction guaranteed or else the cost of books is returned):

_____ *Sweet Fire* @ $19.95
_____ *Weary Warriors* @ $13.95
_____ *Bored Readers Don't Pray Much* @ $15.00

Name_____

Address_____

City _____State _____ Zip _____-____

Telephone _____

E-mail address _____

Sales Tax: Please add 4.25% for orders sent toVirginia.

Postage & handling: 1 book - $3, 2-3 books - $4, 4-5 books -$6

Payment: (circle which one): check, credit card—Visa or MasterCard

Card number: _____Exp. date: ___/___

Name on card: _____

Majesty Publishers

Quick Order Form

Fax orders: 1-703-669-6738. Send this form.

Telephone orders: 1-703-669-6737 Have credit card ready.

Internet orders: Go to www.majestypublishers.com.

Postal orders: Majesty Publishers, P.O. Box 1623, Leesburg, VA 20177, USA.

Questions: E-mail us at majestypub@adelphia.net.

Please indicate quantity wanted of the following books (satisfaction guaranteed or else the cost of books is returned):

_____ *Sweet Fire* @ $19.95
_____ *Weary Warriors* @ $13.95
_____ *Bored Readers Don't Pray Much* @ $15.00

Name_____

Address_____

City _____State _____ Zip _____-____

Telephone _____

E-mail address _____

Sales Tax: Please add 4.25% for orders sent to Virginia.

Postage & handling: 1 book - $3, 2-3 books - $4, 4-5 books -$6

Payment: (circle which one): check, credit card—Visa or MasterCard

Card number: _____Exp. date: ___/___

Name on card: _____

Majesty Publishers

Quick Order Form

Fax orders: 1-703-669-6738. Send this form.

Telephone orders: 1-703-669-6737 Have credit card ready.

Internet orders: Go to www.majestypublishers.com.

Postal orders: Majesty Publishers, P.O. Box 1623, Leesburg, VA 20177, USA.

Questions: E-mail us at majestypub@adelphia.net.

Please indicate quantity wanted of the following books (satisfaction guaranteed or else the cost of books is returned):

_____ *Sweet Fire* @ $19.95
_____ *Weary Warriors* @ $13.95
_____ *Bored Readers Don't Pray Much* @ $15.00

Name_____

Address_____

City _____State _____ Zip _____-____

Telephone _____

E-mail address _____

Sales Tax: Please add 4.25% for orders sent to Virginia.

Postage & handling: 1 book - $3, 2-3 books - $4, 4-5 books -$6

Payment: (circle which one): check, credit card—Visa or MasterCard

Card number: _____Exp. date: ___/___

Name on card: _____

Printed in the United States
1247000004B/55-510

9 780963 328342